STUCK?

Break Free *(At Last!)*
from the Confining Mindsets that Keep You from God's Best

Stan Simmons

Foursquare Media

STUCK?

Published by FOURSQUARE MEDIA
1910 W. Sunset Blvd.
Los Angeles, CA 90026
www.foursquaremedia.org

ISBN 978-0-9802392-5-6
Copyright 2008 by
Printed in the United States of America

Dedication

I am deeply grateful to have spent the major part of my adult life serving a congregation that is determined to be more like Jesus. We have experienced the best of life and the worst of life—together. My relationship with Christ has been shaped in front of them. They are to be commended for their patience and grace as they have listened to me muse over Scripture these many years. Together we have come to believe that we can, and must, make a difference for Jesus because *eternity is at stake*.

With deep gratitude and respect I dedicate this book to my friends at Faith Chapel!

Contents

Introduction   **7**

Chapter One:
Don't Get Stuck in the Past   **11**

Chapter Two:
Don't Get Stuck in Fear   **23**

Chapter Three:
Don't Get Stuck on Yourself   **37**

Chapter Four:
Don't Get Stuck in Your Thinking   **49**

Chapter Five:
Don't Get Stuck on the World   **63**

Chapter Six:
Don't Get Stuck in the Book   **75**

Chapter Seven:
Don't Get Stuck in an Experience   **87**

Chapter Eight:
Don't Get Stuck in the Huddle   **99**

Chapter Nine:
Unstuck: Life with a Purpose   **111**

Introduction

You're sitting in your favorite chair in front of the TV, watching an action movie that has you by the throat.

Suddenly, just as the plot thickens and the music crescendos, crazy images—colorful, but strange and distorted—appear on the screen. The actors begin to speak and move in weird, jerky slow-motion, like aliens from a 50s sci-fi flick. Then everything freezes.

The DVD is stuck! It falters a bit, stuck then unstuck, stuck then unstuck. Finally you give up, get out of your easy chair, eject the DVD, and do your best to clean it. Then you try again—and again and again—to advance the movie past the sticking point. Only to be frustrated.

A defective DVD is bad enough. But what if it's not a movie? What if the picture freezes in the middle of real life?

It's happened to all of us, hasn't it? It seems to be part of the human experience. We get stalled out in old habits, old haunts, old fears, and old ruts in the road. We come to what feels like a dead-end in our careers, our marriages, or our spiritual lives. We may feel bored, unfulfilled, locked into a set of life circumstances that just don't seem to be going anywhere.

We're S-T-U-C-K.

That's what happened to the DVD of my life when I was about twenty-five years old. I'd been raised in a strong Christian home, but had chosen to go my own way. After ten years of rebellion against God and everything I'd been brought up to believe, my life seemed to be coming unraveled. I was lonely, depressed, unfulfilled, and confused. I'd done things in that period of time I would have previously thought unimaginable. I was stuck—and deeply unhappy—in a very dark place.

But never underestimate the power of prayer to tow a life—any life—out of the ditch. My parents and loved ones had prayed for me long and faithfully, without much evidence that God had heard them.

But He had.

And in His time, things began to move.

I woke up one bright sunshiny morning, alone in my little apartment, with the overwhelming sense of God's presence in the room. Without even thinking, I found myself sliding out of bed onto my knees, crying out to God. I can remember my prayer to this day. I said, "Please Lord, if You'll forgive me, I'll go anyplace You want me to go, and do anything You ask me to do."

And just that quickly, I found traction and rolled out of those deep ruts I'd been spinning my tires in for years. I was unstuck!

The next Sunday, my bride-to-be and I were in church. I knew that if I wanted a new start, attending church would be essential to my spiritual growth. We not only showed up for church, but also attended a young adult Sunday school class. There we were: two confused, nervous, but well-intentioned young adults who were trying to find their way. But as it turned out, no one in that church seemed to feel any inclination to help us. They were caught up in their own world, their own friendships, and Ginger and I just didn't seem to fit in.

As I look back on it now, it's interesting to me that during a time when God was pursuing us, I felt like the people in that church wanted to distance themselves from us.

After a few weeks, we tried another church. With a very different result. There was nothing in the least impressive about this second church: not the building, the people, the music, nor the preaching. But at the conclusion of the service, the pastor met us at the back door. I'll never forget his large, rough hands; he worked on a construction job because the church couldn't afford to pay him a salary. Neither will I ever forget what he said to us. He grabbed my hand, looked me in the eye, and said, "We need people like you here."

Imagine how those words sounded to us in that moment. We'd been searching, had felt shunned, but now this man was reaching out to us. And God was reaching out through Him.

We were unstuck and on our way.

Perhaps because I know what it's like to be stuck, I have great compassion for people in the same condition. It's always our choice, isn't it? When we recognize we're in a tough place, we can either stay there or we can make good decisions that will help us move on.

In my years of ministry I've seen people who were stuck in all kinds of real-life situations. And it is my passion to help them get unstuck so they can move toward everything God created them to be.

We all want our lives to matter. It's part of our DNA. At the same time, however, we all face obstacles along the way, roadblocks to reaching our full potential. Though well intentioned, most of us tend to stall out at some point in our journey. Maybe you're stuck right now, not sure whether you should call a tow truck or play a game of solitaire on the dashboard.

Let's spend some time together thinking about some of the major ways people get bogged down along the way. Busyness, crisis, recreation, the demands of family, and church life can so easily overwhelm us and become the focus of our lives. Even wonderful Christian endeavors can consume us and become obstacles to our making the difference we really want to make; and of course, sin, our past, or fear can cause us to get stuck.

I invite you to spend some quality time in the pages of this little book, pondering the challenges associated with being stuck...and experiencing the freedom and joy of getting unstuck!

Chapter One

Don't Get Stuck in the Past

A number of years ago, I attended my fortieth high school class reunion.

Now for some, that prospect might seem about as enticing as a root canal. But for whatever reason, I found myself looking forward to the gathering with anticipation. In fact, for months ahead of time I started contacting old chums from high school and renewing our friendship. I hadn't been in touch with these people for years, but now felt compelled to catch up on old times.

When the reunion finally arrived, however, I had all the apprehensions you might expect. *Would people recognize me? Would anyone want to talk to me?* Happily, my fears were soon set aside, and I actually had a very good time chatting with a number of people. Over the next couple of days it was fun getting reacquainted, reminiscing a bit, and catching up with what old friends had done with their lives.

That process, of course, triggered more than a few

long-shelved memories—some good, some not so good. As much as I enjoyed living in the past for a few days, I finally came to the conclusion that high school was then, and this is now.

And I like now.

I like now very much.

In the days leading up to the reunion, Ginger and I had an interesting conversation. It was probably after dinner, while we were cleaning up in the kitchen. That's where a good many of our more profound dialogues have taken place.

"If you were to choose the favorite time of your life," she asked me, "what would that be?"

I thought about it, but only for a moment.

"Right now," I said.

But what would Ginger choose? When I asked, she hesitated only a moment. "I guess I would have to say, 'right now,' too."

What a wonderful thing to be able to say, "*Right now, is the greatest time of my life.*" (Which enables you, by the way, to get up in the morning and say—perhaps after a cup of coffee—"Today is the greatest day of my life.")

In recent years I've heard myself say on numerous occasions, "*These* are the good old days!" What a contrast to looking back into the past and saying, "If only things could be like that again. I was so happy *then.*"

You probably know someone like a high school friend of mine. He's good looking, has a winsome personality, and was one of the most popular kids in school. You know the type: quarterback on the football team, captain of the basketball team, and a track star to boot. He worked as a lifeguard at the swimming pool in the summertime (with a great build and a perfect tan to show for it), and seemed to have everything going for him.

We renewed our friendship at a birthday party recently. Primarily due to his congenial personality, we picked up as though we had been friends all our lives, without interruption.

But as we talked it dawned on me: *This guy's living in the past.*

In other words, he was stuck.

When we were talking about days gone by, he was laughing, smiling, and filled with enthusiasm. But when I tried to steer the conversation toward current events, he became hesitant, with little or nothing to say. Life for him, I began to suspect, was all about "the way it used to be."

The more we talked, the more I became convinced that was true. I discovered that he has a room filled with memorabilia from our high school days, spends a great deal of his time in the town where we were raised, is still involved in athletic activities there, and stays in close contact with friends from the "good old days."

Is there anything wrong with that?

Well...yes and no. Of course, it's a very good thing to have fond memories of the past and to enjoy lifelong friendships, but life moves on...and my friend hasn't. His eyes are so fixed on the perceived glories in his rearview mirror that he has no time or inclination to think about where he is at the moment. Or where he might be headed.

Stuck in Reverse

What is it that mires a person down in the past? For my friend, it was that vague feeling that life could never be as good as it once was, when he was at the top of his game and king on the hill. He was stuck in the good times—or what he now imagines to be the good times.

But that's not the only reason we get our gears locked in reverse. Sometimes we're stuck in the past, not because it was so good, but because it was so *bad*. We can't get beyond certain traumatic or hurtful experiences in our lives.

After pastoring the same church for over thirty years, I can look back at some times and places in my ministry where I could have, very easily, become stuck—and probably would have, but for the kindness and grace of God that enabled me to make different choices.

One afternoon I came home from work early, desperate over a conflict I was having with two staff members. These were more than colleagues—they were friends, people I loved. But somehow we had come to a place of deep misunderstanding—to the point where they decided to quit their jobs and leave the church.

When I arrived home, I found my youngest daughter, who had just graduated from high school, packing her car. She had decided to move to the Oregon Coast to live with an aunt, and Ginger and I were both very grieved over the circumstances under which she was leaving.

I will never forget that day. I found myself bent over the sink, throwing up, in such turmoil I thought I was going to lose my mind.

Later that afternoon I turned to my wife and said, "I can't do this anymore. I'm going to leave the church."

I'll never forget what she said to me. "Stan, if you leave now, Satan will beat you up with this for the rest of your life."

She was right, of course. If we had left then we would not have remembered the great blessing and growth we had experienced in the church to that point. We wouldn't have remembered those who had come to Christ under our ministry, or continued to celebrate those whose marriages had been saved and whose lives were turned around. What we *would* have remembered—through all our days—was the traumatic experience that drove us away. And I seriously doubt that we would still be in pastoral ministry today.

We could have become stuck, but by God's grace, we didn't. We were able to learn the tough lessons He sought to teach us, and move on.

Stuck for Life

I've seen people stall out, becoming stuck in the past, for a variety of reasons. My own brother, who now suffers from dementia, got stuck in the past a number of years ago because of a change at the local library. He was very bright, well educated, and an avid reader who used the library often. One day he went to his beloved refuge only to discover that the card catalog drawers had been replaced with computer terminals.

Intimidated by computers and irritated at the new trend to computerize, he walked out the door of the library, vowing to never to return.

And he never did.

Even though he'd been offered help and tutoring, he refused to reconsider. He was stuck. Tight. And sad to say, he *chose* to be stuck. Who knows what the stimulation of learning to use the computer, the Internet, and e-mail might have meant for his ongoing mental state. But he chose to nurture what he considered an offense, and that decision would color the rest of his days.

As a pastor, I've seen people get stuck on liturgy, dress styles, preaching styles, building projects, but most of all (God help us), music! A dear friend of mine, who listened to my daily radio broadcast for years but had never attended our church, finally talked her husband into visiting a service. He was reluctant, but her persuasiveness won the day.

It was a Saturday evening, and as I walked into the worship center, there they were, sitting by the aisle toward the back. Of course I was delighted to see them. For the next several weeks, I watched for them, and they were always seated in the same place.

And then they disappeared and never came back.

I saw my friend a few months later, and chose not to ask her why they had stopped attending. But she told me anyway, as I knew she would. And I was shocked at her answer. Her husband had told her, "I will not go to a church where they have *drums.*"

Well, lots of churches now have drums. In the past, they didn't. But now they do.

This couple had actually loved our fellowship, valued the teaching, and perhaps could even visualize themselves getting involved…but he got stuck over a music preference. (And she got stuck with his bad decision.)

People tend to choose music styles according to the generation in which they first started attending church; some are stuck in the '70s, '80s, or '90s, and frankly, some will get stuck where they are right now.

Imagine how many people are bogged down and have stopped growing spiritually over issues as trivial as "how people dress." I heard a pastor recently refer to jeans as "the devil's pants." He was quoting people in his part of the country who find it distasteful for people to wear jeans to church. *As if God cares.*

So how can we get unstuck?

If your car is stuck in the snow on some back mountain road, one of the first things you want to consider is finding a flat piece of wood to wedge under the affected tires. That may give you enough traction to go forward (or back up) enough to get yourself out of trouble. Let me suggest a couple of ideas that might offer the extra torque you need to power out of your particular life situation.

Traction Finders

Look back

Could I encourage you to review your past, and as best you can, determine what may be holding you up? Be blatantly honest with yourself: is there any residual of anger, bitterness, disappointment, or hurt? Or maybe you have fallen prey to the temptation to hold on to good times, and that has prevented you from living in the here and now. If you're anything like most of us, there is no shortage of things that can get a hook in you and hinder your advancement toward becoming everything God has for you.

Express your heart to the Lord

What are your emotions toward those things that seem to have tripped you up? Do you feel like giving up? Do you want to let go and move forward but don't know how? Tell Him about it. He's interested. You would really be surprised *how* interested.

Remember the story of Cain? This firstborn of all humanity got stuck in a deep, slippery rut of resentment and jealousy. Never mind the reasons. Suffice it to say he was in up to his axles, and in great spiritual danger.

That's why God intervened. The Bible says Cain was "both dejected and very angry, and his face grew dark with fury. 'Why are you angry?' the Lord asked him. 'Why is your face so dark with rage? It can be bright with joy if you will do what you should! But if you refuse to obey, watch out. Sin is waiting to attack you, longing to destroy you. But you can conquer it!'" (Genesis 4:5-7, TLB).

If only Cain had taken the opportunity to express his feelings to God in that critical season of his life. He had an open invitation! Obviously God already knew what was troubling him, and was ready to discuss the issue. But Cain locked all of that poison up in his own soul, and the next thing we read about him, he was killing his brother, Abel.

If you are angry, even with the Lord, *tell* Him about it. Guess what...He knows already! Obviously you want to communicate with the Lord with the deepest sense of respect, but let's be honest here: He created you, and He understands your emotions and thoughts toward difficult issues. Is there anyone you need to pray for? Is there a situation you need to bring before the Lord and examine with Him? Ask Him to help you. Do you feel absolutely stuck in the mud? Ask Him to throw you a rope. He will! That is the great desire of His heart.

Trust God for your future

Whatever your age, your past, or your current station in life, God isn't through with you. What did you used to dream about? What are the God-given visions you've simply given up on—or perhaps lost along the way? Go back, take a fresh grip on that dream, and allow it to rekindle what you once contended for.

Perhaps you've taken a difficult path, a path you wouldn't have chosen in a thousand years. There have been hurts, disappointments, and times of failure. But now you have the opportunity to put all of that under His control, trust that He has your life in His hands, and is fully able to get you where He wants you to be. God really does know what He's doing, you know.

A number of years ago, I went through a period of severe burnout, and decided to seek counseling. After two weeks of some pretty intense sessions, one of my counselors asked me a rather simple question: "Stan, what does your future look like?"

He might as well have asked me the median September temperature on Neptune. I had no idea what to say. At that moment, I didn't have a clue. I had gone through several deep disappointments in a short period of time, I was stuck, and couldn't seem to get past what I had experienced. As a result, I had completely lost sight of the future—and really didn't even want to think about it.

His question stirred in me for several weeks, and finally I was able to get my eyes off of the past and begin to dream about the future God had for me.

To remind me to keep my eyes focused in that direction, I placed two large glass jars on my desk, one full of marbles. I began with enough marbles to represent one marble for every day over a ten-year period. (That's a lot of marbles!) Each day I move a marble from one jar to the other as a physical reminder that I have a limited amount of time on this earth, and that I want to use my time wisely.

One of the things I say each day is, "Lord, let's build a great future together."

Open your hand

As you are reading these words, take one of your hands and make it into a tight fist. Go ahead, try it. Imagine that you are gripping whatever it is that has you stuck in the past. So you're physically holding onto this thing, knuckles tight and white, for dear life.

Now, stop and think about the consequences of that clenched fist. Do you want to remain stuck, never attaining what God has for you? Of course not! So, how long are you going to hold on? When are you going to relax those fingers and…let go?

My wife met with a friend a number of years ago, a woman who wasn't enjoying life very much, to say the least. This woman (we'll call her Crystal) was angry, bitter, and very negative about most everything in life. As Ginger talked with her, it became clear that she had a lot of unforgiveness toward people who throughout her life had offended or hurt her in some way. And the list was rather long.

As Ginger probed further, she discovered that Crystal had gone so far as to *keep a file folder full of reminders* (I kid you not) of how and when people had wounded her. Occasionally, she would go back and review these detailed reminders, allowing herself the "luxury" of steeping in all that bitterness and bile. Ginger was shocked to find names, dates, and specifics about what had brought hurt to her friend's life.

They prayed together, and Ginger encouraged her to throw the file in the fireplace, which she did. As a consequence, with God's willing help, she became unstuck and freed from her past.

Maybe it would have never occurred to you to keep a file folder full of people's past offenses. But do you have any mental file folders? Do you have a list of offenses tucked away somewhere in your memory? It's really not that much different than having a physical folder, is it? Either way, the files have to be extracted and shredded if you want to climb out of the unhappy rut in which you may find yourself.

Now take that tightly clenched fist you made a moment ago and begin to relax it. Open it up, finger by finger, until you can see the palm of your hand. In the same way, God can help you let go of that which you've been clinging to. From this point forward, let me encourage you to look to the future, and break the habit of continually looking over your shoulder. If your past tries to work its way back into your thinking, close your fist, think about the consequences of holding onto your past, and open your hand again. Let it go!

Reap the joyous benefits of getting your life in motion again.

Chapter Two

Don't Get Stuck in Fear

When I was growing up, basketball was a high calling for me. I spent endless hours at our neighborhood tennis court, shooting hoops. Come to think of it, I don't remember if I ever saw anyone playing tennis in that place...but there was always a game of shirts and skins going. Then there were the hours in our driveway, practicing my shooting until far after dark. I wouldn't let myself quit until I made ten free throws in a row.

I pled with God that He would let me grow to at least six feet tall so I could play on a basketball team. Little did I know just how tall I *really* needed to be to have a realistic chance at fulfilling my dreams.

Finally in the seventh grade, I got to go out for a real team. One day during warm-ups I was practicing the two-handed set shot, my specialty. Apparently, the coach had been watching. After running us through our drills, he picked two teams for a scrimmage.

Just before play began, he pulled the whistle out of his mouth and called me over to talk to him.

"Simmons," he said, looking me in the eyes, "I want you to shoot your shot, that two-handed set shot."

Shoot my shot? MY shot? Who would have thought my big chance would come so soon? This was my opportunity to do what I knew I was completely competent to do: sink a simple set shot from fifteen feet. With my heart in my throat, I ran onto the court, caught the ball, and called on my body to follow through with the simple action I had practiced for countless hours.

But I couldn't do it.

I was frozen with fear.

I could do the drills and sink my shot in practice when no one of significance was watching, but when the game started, fans were present, or the coach was looking at me, it was like I'd never touched a basketball in my life. I froze, stuck in a paralyzing fear.

According to some phobia experts, over 7,000 fears have been classified and named. Most of us can identify in some measure with at least a dozen of them: fear of being alone, darkness, failure, flying, heights, public speaking, or spiders. A number of others, however, were new to me: fear of chickens (*chickens?*), chopsticks, crossing the street, feeling pleasure, flutes, hearing good news, kissing, relatives, responsibility, being touched, being infested by worms, and (my favorite), the fear of peanut butter sticking to the roof of your mouth…*arachibutyrophobia.*

These are the folks, I suppose, who have to avoid the peanut butter aisle at the local grocery store. One glimpse of a jar of Skippy Extra-Crunchy and…well, who knows what might happen?

There are, of course, healthy fears.

One of my favorite places to visit is The Little Grand Canyon of Yellowstone, in Yellowstone National Park. Look up some images on the Internet. It's spectacular. As you approach the edge of the canyon, there are warning signs everywhere, cautioning people not to get to close to that sheer drop-off, or allow leave their children unattended. But every time I've been there, I've seen little ones walk right up to the edge, with no parent in sight.

Rather foolish, I would say. A fear of heights can motivate us to stay away from dangerous situations, and remind us to keep a close eye on protecting our loved ones.

The appropriate fear of God is a healthy fear. Notice the following real-life benefits:

The fear of the LORD is the beginning of wisdom….
(Psalm 111:10)

The fear of the LORD adds length to life….
(Proverbs 10:27)

The fear of the LORD is a fountain of life….
(Proverbs 14:27)

The fear of the LORD teaches a man wisdom….
(Proverbs 15:33)

…Through the fear of the LORD a man avoid evil.
(Proverbs 16:6)

The fear of the LORD leads to life:
then one rests content, untouched by trouble.
(Proverbs 19:23)

When Solomon uses the word "fear" in these passages, he's talking about a profound respect and bone-deep, reverential awe. Growing up in a Christian home, I experienced both a healthy and an unhealthy fear of God. I remember the horror of thinking Jesus had already returned, and I had somehow been "left behind." I can clearly recall standing in church during the invitation at the end of the service, when the pastor would invite people to come to the front and give their lives to Jesus. I wanted to, but I was so terrified my hands would grip the back of the pew in front of me until I trembled.

That was an illogical, unhealthy fear.

As a young adult, I ran from God for years, afraid of what He would do to me because I was running. But I kept running and running. That too was illogical and unhealthy.

After I gave my life to Jesus Christ, the worst thought in the world to me was ever becoming separated from a heavenly Father who loved me and had sent His own Son to rescue me.

It's still the worst thought in the world.

And it is a healthy fear.

Healthy fear motivates us in positive ways, protecting us from danger or harm. Unhealthy fear keeps us from advancing and becoming everything God created us to be. It stifles, hinders, gets us stuck, and uses all of its influence to keep us stuck.

"I Will Help You Speak…"

A number of years ago, I took a personality inventory that not only described my temperament but identified me with a Bible character who owned a similar temperament. That biblical personality happened to be Moses.

The Bible speaks of a crucial moment when God commissioned Moses, at that time an elderly shepherd in the Midian desert, to confront the king of Egypt and lead His people into the promised land. Though God has chosen Moses and demonstrated His commitment to act on his behalf, Moses was afraid, paralyzed to even contemplate such a thing.

Notice these words toward the conclusion of their conversation in Exodus chapter 4:

> "Moses said to the LORD, 'O LORD, I have never been eloquent, neither in the past nor since you have spoken to your servant. I am slow of speech and tongue.' The LORD said to him, 'Who gave man his mouth? Who makes him deaf or mute? Who gives him sight or makes him blind? Is it not I, the LORD? Now go; I will help you speak and will teach you what to say." (vv. 11-12)

This incident is very meaningful to me. In fact, it changed my life. I had known for a long time that God was calling me into full time ministry, but I had been axle-deep in a rut of fear, terrified of public speaking.

Unwilling to face my fears, I had refused to do

oral reports in school, preferring to take a lower grade than stand in front of my classmates. In college, I even changed majors to avoid taking a speech class.

But the time came when I had to face that fear once and for all, or remain stuck for the rest of my life. Was I going to be God's man and obey Him, or would I allow myself to be mired down through all the years of my short life on this world?

At some point, push had to come to shove.

I remember so well sitting in the lobby of the church Ginger and I attended at the time, wrestling with God over the call on my life, when I came upon the passage that records this incident in Moses' life. When I read these words, *"Now go; I will help you speak and will teach you what to say,"* they leapt off the page at me. I knew God was speaking to me as surely as He had spoken to Moses.

Through that experience and the incidents that would follow, I learned a principle that has served me well through all my days: *Courage is not the absence of fear; courage is moving forward in spite of your fear.*

I used to believe that if someone had courage, that meant he or she wasn't afraid, period. But I have since learned that courageous people are those who move forward *in spite* of their fear. I didn't overcome my terror of public speaking in an instant; I overcame over the long haul, by consistently confronting that fear and not letting it hold me back.

Shortly after the experience I described above, I was given the opportunity to speak in our church's Sunday morning services. Our pastor was leaving town for a few days and invited me to bring a message in multiple services that weekend.

I was, of course, terrified.

I remember lying on the floor in the pastor's office, crying out to God, begging Him not to make me go out there and get in front of all those people. But it was fifteen minutes before the service, and who else was going to do it?

I can close my eyes right now and see Ginger, sitting in one of the front pews in the congregation, as I stepped out onto the platform. Pale and filled with fear for me, her hands were literally trembling. She was shaking on the outside, I was shaking on the inside.

I wish I could give some impressive testimony about God immediately taking away my fear, and allowing me to speak like Jack Hayford. But that wasn't my experience. Rather than delivering me from all my fear, what He enabled me to do was preach *through* my fear. In other words, I had to look my fear in the eye and move forward, still afraid. But I learned, through many experiences like the one I just described, that God was faithful to His promise. *"Now go; I will help you speak and will teach you what to say."*

So, what are you afraid of? What stops you in your tracks?

Are you willing to face your fears, whatever they may be? Are you willing to move forward, in courage, and overcome what has held you back, kept you from advancing toward what God wants you to become?

Let me suggest a simple acrostic to help us move forward together: Are you ready for some C.O.U.R.A.G.E.?

<u>C</u>learly Identify What Frightens You

Maybe you've never done that. Maybe you have never specifically named the apprehension that has its hooks in your soul. What is it? What's holding you back? If those phobia experts are right, and there are over 7,000 named and classified fears, only two are *innate*, fears that we are born with: the fear of falling, and the fear of loud noises. The rest we learn.

So...*name* your fear. Look it in the eye, and pin it down. Just what is it that you're afraid of? Just what kind of mud are stuck in?

<u>O</u>bserve Where You Have Placed Your Trust

The story of David and Goliath begins, as you may recall, by identifying the fact that when Goliath came out and challenged the army of Israel, Saul and his trained soldiers were scared stiff (or maybe I should say, "scared stuck").

Then along came David, a teenage boy who had some skill with a sling and a stone, but had never had so much as ten minutes' training as a soldier. He said, in essence, "What's wrong with you people? Are you going to allow this guy to intimidate the people of God? Bring him on. *I'll* fight him if you won't!" David took responsibility, stepped up to the plate, and faced the man others were afraid to face, in the belief that God would deliver him.

And He did. Did He ever!

For all of David's practice with his little sling out

in the lonely wilderness, it wasn't his weapons that gave him courage that day. It was his confidence in the Lord. *"You come against me with sword and spear and javelin, but I come against you in the name of the Lord Almighty."* [1]

Was David afraid? Of course he was. But this wasn't the first challenge he'd encountered in his young life. He had already seen the faithfulness of God in enabling him to face lions and bears while protecting his sheep. If God helped had him then, why wouldn't He help him now?

He would. And He did.

Where is your trust? I have learned never to compare myself and my abilities with what I face, but to always compare what I face with God, and His abilities.

Understand This: God Has a Plan for You

I love the word of encouragement God gave Jeremiah to help him overcome fear.

> "Before I formed you in the womb I knew you, before you were born I set you apart." [2]

Can you hear the trepidation in the young prophet's voice as he responds?

> "I don't know how to speak; I am only a child." [3]

In response, the Lord gave Jeremiah a new perspective on how to think about himself. He bolstered the prophet's confidence by reassuring Jeremiah that he would never be alone, that God would always be there for him.

> "Do not say, 'I am only a child.' You must go to everyone I send you to and will say whatever I command you. Do not be afraid, for I am with you and will rescue you." [4]

Whose evaluation of you is the most important: yours, someone else's, or God's? I suggest that to have a healthy and accurate view of yourself, you must learn to see yourself as God sees you.

Recognize that God is with You

In the eighth grade my classmates selected me to give a welcome speech at our graduation ceremony. The prospect of standing in front of teachers, parents, and friends for such an occasion turned my very bones into Jell-O.

Shortly after I was given the bad news, I bumped into Mr. Grosnickle, one of the most popular teachers in the school, out in the hall. He congratulated me on my selection as class speaker, but it soon became obvious that I wasn't nearly as excited about it as he was. I don't remember exactly what I said to him, but he got the idea. I was encased in a granite block of sheer terror.

He put his arm around me, and as we walked down the hall, he said, "Stan, they wouldn't have selected you to give that speech if you weren't qualified to do it. Of course you can do it!" He then gave me several suggestions on how to put a speech together, and pointed me toward some helpful reference material.

Bolstered by that encouragement, I went home and frantically put a speech together. His kind, timely words got me unstuck! (At least for the moment.)

As much as we can benefit from the encouragement of others, however, what we need most is an ear to hear such words from the God who loves us. If you could picture God Himself walking alongside you, would that make a difference in how you view your worst fears? Of course it would! And here are some of the words He would probably be saying to you:

> *"So do not fear, for I am with you; do not be dismayed, for I am your God. I will strengthen you and help you; I will uphold you with my righteous right hand."* [5]

The amazing truth about you, communicated in Psalm 139, is that:

> God knew you before you were born.
> He created you and did a great job.
> He has a plan for your life.
> He knows when you sit down and when you stand up.
> He knows what you are thinking right now.
> He knows what you are going to say, before you say it.
> He knows when you go to bed at night and when you get up in the morning.
> He is behind you, before you, beside you.
> His hand is guiding you and holding you fast.

Advance toward What You Fear

Yes, that's right, go ahead and make your move. Move *toward* that thing that paralyzes you, not away from it. That is the only way you will overcome your fear: look it in the eye, and in God's grace and strength, defy it!

I remember walking into the convention center to speak at our denomination's international convention. I had prepared for weeks, but now, as I waited for my moment to step up the podium, my mind kept jumping, freezing, and skipping around like that defective DVD I mentioned in the introduction.

I was as well prepared as I knew how to be, but all of those old fears kept threatening to rise up again and overwhelm me. Was I really going to be stuck, at this important moment in my life?

Go Ahead…Step Across that Line

As you face your fear and advance toward it, everything in you—your doubts, your emotions, your negative thoughts, your history, your perception of yourself—screams out, telling you to stop, to go back, or to freeze into position like the proverbial deer in the headlights.

But you can't stop—not if you're going to overcome. You must cross that line where there is no turning back. That is the moment of victory, when you can honestly say, "I will not let my fears hold me back."

When I stepped up to the lectern at the convention center, looked out across several hundred fellow pastors and their families, took a deep breath asking for God's help, and began to speak…the DVD came unstuck. My mind cleared, and I began to declare the words that I knew very well God had given me.

With His help, I looked my fears in the eye, stepped forward, and experienced a colossal victory.

<u>E</u>xpress Your Gratitude for God's Help

An amazing thing happens when you face your fears and put all of those feelings of foreboding into their proper perspective. You are unstuck! The spinning wheels begin to find traction. The tread bites into the slippery turf and something truly wondrous occurs.

You begin to move forward.

When that happens, don't forget to say, "Thank you" to the Lord. Remember, He is the one who gave you courage. And simply acknowledging what He had done will solidify that decision.

Thousands of times now, while waiting to get up and speak, whether in the church I pastor, or elsewhere, I stop at some point and say to the Lord, "Thank You for helping me today, and thank You for helping me overcome my fears."

Unstuck! What freedom!

Chapter Three

Don't Get Stuck on Yourself

As Rich and I headed downstairs in the church to get a folding table, Michael, Rich's five-year-old, was right on our heels. My friend and I were setting up for a women's Bible study the following morning.

Arriving at the closet at the bottom of the stairs, I opened the door and reached up to pull on the string attached to the light bulb, flooding the little room with light.

Moving toward the back of the closet where the tables were stored, I bent over to avoid bumping my head on the low ceiling. But before I could put my hands on one of the tables, the light blinked out.

Could it be the bulb?

But then the light blinked on again, and I could see Michael, a grin on his impish little face and the string in his hand, ready to pull the switch again. The light flashed off, then on, then off. Then I could hear his dad's firm command, "Michael, turn on that light and *leave it alone.*"

Rich picked up one end of the table, I lifted the other, and we headed out of the closet. I shut the closet door, and we moved toward the stairway. As we were maneuvering the table up the stairs, I heard a noise beside me, turned, and there was Michael on the other side of the table, both hands firmly underneath, "helping" us muscle the table toward the sanctuary. He might have gotten his little fingers pinched, but how could I reprimand him? He was such a cute little guy.

Soon we reached the top of the stairs and headed across the sanctuary. When we reached the other side we set the table on its side, extended the legs, locked them, and put it on its feet.

I reached down to get the coffee urn, and set it up on the table. But the table already had a centerpiece. There was Michael, grinning again, standing in the middle of the table, flexing his little muscles like Charles Atlas.

Michael was very proud of himself for his involvement in getting the table upstairs and in place. Obviously, he overestimated his contribution.

But the more I thought about it, the more I had to laugh. How often do you and I do the same thing? We face an overwhelming task, humbly pleading with God for help, then take all the credit when the accolades are being passed out.

I can't tell you how many times I have walked through the worship center crying out for God's help with the weekend message, only to take the credit in the hallway when someone says, "Great job, pastor."

Pride is insidious. It lurks in the wings, waiting to slither into our thoughts and manifest itself. While it may begin in small, insignificant ways, it is never satisfied. Once pride has a foothold it clamors for more, until it finally convinces us that we are adequate in our own strength, no longer need God, and can do quite well on our own, thank you.

I used to regard myself as a humble person, until one day I heard the whisper of the Holy Spirit, *You are proud of your humility.* Ouch!

Pride will stunt your spiritual growth and development. If you allow it to remain welcome in your thoughts, you will face serious consequences.

Stuck?

Oh yes, but worse than that, you will be opposed by God Himself.[6]

An Old Testament story gives the account of a man who was given an unforgettable lesson in humility. Naaman was a great man, highly respected, a valiant soldier, and commander of the army of Aram. But he had leprosy.[7]

If you aren't familiar with leprosy, it's a disease that, once contracted, will literally eat away your flesh. Eventually, it will kill you, but not until it has deformed you in tragic ways.

The Bible account tells of a young Israeli slave girl who served Naaman's wife. One day she said (probably with a sigh), "If only my master would see the prophet who is in Samaria! He would cure him of his leprosy" (2 Kings 5:3).

Visit a prophet in hated Israel? It's not likely a prospect that would have appealed to the proud military commander under anything approaching normal conditions. But these weren't normal conditions. And when you're desperate, all options are on the table.

Receiving his king's permission to visit Israel, he arrived at Elisha's humble residence. Now everything about this royal visitor should have impressed the prophet—his attire, his entourage, and his horses and chariots. It all communicated, "I am a very important man, and I have condescended to call on you in person." Try to imagine a shiny black stretch limo pulling up to your front door, escorted by half a dozen motorcycle cops, blue lights flashing.

But the man of God wasn't impressed in the least.

In fact, he didn't even go to the door to speak to General Naaman.

Elisha's servant met the Syrian VIP at the door with a message that the great man didn't like at all: "Go and wash yourself seven times in the Jordan River, and you will be healed."

Deeply offended by this prescription, Naaman spluttered, "'I thought that he would surely come out to me and stand and call on the name of the LORD his God, wave his hand over the spot and cure me of my leprosy. Are not Abana and Pharpar, the rivers of Damascus, better than any of the waters of Israel? Couldn't I wash in them and be cleansed?' So he turned and went off in a rage" (2 Kings 5:11-12).

In other words, Naaman had his own ideas and expectations for this encounter with a prophet of the living God. He wanted to administrate his own healing, stage-manage his own miracle. He went off in a snit, potentially stuck by his pride.

But here's the point: The wheels of Naaman's luxury chariot may have turned around and around as he drove away from Elisha's house, *but he was stuck.*

Stuck in his disease. Stuck in his leprosy. Stuck with a death sentence. Stuck in his pride.

Then we see these words, recorded in Scripture:

> Naaman's servants went to him and said, "My father, if the prophet had told you to do some great thing, would you not have done it? How much more, then, when he tells you, 'Wash and be cleansed!'"

> So he went down and dipped himself in the Jordan seven times, as the man of God had told him, and his flesh was restored and became clean like that of a young boy. (2 Kings 5:13-14)

God required humility of this proud man. The Lord's request had been simple, but humbling—in Naaman's eyes, humiliating.

Has God ever asked you to do something that was humbling, perhaps even, humiliating?

The Girl on the Stairway

I was sitting in the quiet sanctuary, praying and reviewing the message for the weekend services, when I heard a knock on the front door of the church.

I ignored it at first, knowing the doors were locked. This was my one place of refuge from the busyness of a church office. I often walked across the parking lot from our administration offices, locked the doors, and enjoyed a few minutes of solitude to do what needed to be done to prepare well for the weekend services.

But then came a second, more insistent knock on the door. Now I was offended. *The nerve! Why can't people leave me alone?* I thought to myself. *After all, I'm the man of God, trying to pray and prepare so I can deliver His Word. Don't they get it?*

I got up and moved quickly toward the door, thrust open the door leading into the lobby, and there he was, across the street putting his briefcase in the trunk of his car. I opened the glass door, put on my best preacherly smile, and called out nicely, "Is there something I can help you with?"

He turned and called out the name of the person he was looking for. I told him, in a cordial tone, where he could find the church office, and he was on his way.

I turned to go back inside, and as soon as the door was shut, my frustration boiled over. Even though he could no longer hear me, I let this guy have it. Verbally. Out loud. In no uncertain terms, I told him what I thought of his inconsiderate interruption, and waste of my valuable time.

Really, I said some things about that stranger that a preacher, or anyone else, should never say. Nothing vile, perhaps, but let me be clear…he was thoroughly rebuked.

When I had vented my frustration to my satisfaction, I decided as long as I was already up, to go downstairs to the restroom. I turned to go down the stairs, and there sat Nora, about halfway down the stairs sitting on the landing. Nora, was a sixteen-year-old high school student who attended our church. She was one of those kids that come along every decade or so—smart, cute, godly, great character; she had it all.

I stood stunned for a moment, as a hot wave of embarrassment swept over me. Had she heard my rant? *Of course* she'd heard, she was only fifteen feet away.

Once again, I put on my finest preacher smile. "Well, hi, Nora! Is there something I can help you with?"

She wasn't smiling, and I thought I could see disappointment on her face. "No, pastor," she said. "I was just waiting for you to finish so I could get into the sanctuary and pray for a few minutes."

I told her I would be through in just a few minutes, and quickly headed down the stairs. I was in anguish, my thoughts racing. *What am I going to do? What will she think of me now? Who will she tell what I said? How am I going to get out of this?*

I walked slowly around the sanctuary, back and forth through the rows of pews, pleading my case to the Lord. After a few minutes, I heard the whisper of the Holy Spirit: *You know, Stan, what bothers Me about you is that you really aren't upset about what you said. You're only upset because Nora HEARD what you said.*

Of course He was exactly right. The sword of the Spirit probed my heart, and in a flash my remorse deepened. And the more I thought about it the worse it got.

I paced and prayed for a few more minutes, knowing I needed to go back and face Nora. But I had no idea what I would say to her or how I could explain my conduct.

I walked out the doors of the sanctuary into the

lobby, turned to go down the stairs, and there she sat. Sitting down beside her on the landing I humbly began to explain, as best I could.

"Nora," I said, "I need to ask for your forgiveness."

She looked at me, eyes wide. I told her what the Lord had shown me about myself, and how disturbed I was by it. We talked for perhaps ten minutes. She of course was gracious and godly, as she always was, but I was humiliated.

It was a great lesson for me, and I'm sure Nora learned some important lessons as well. For one thing, she learned that not only was her pastor imperfect, but that he was willing to humble himself and acknowledge his sorrow to a sixteen-year-old girl.

How about you? Have you ever been asked to do something by the Lord that required humiliation on your part?

Where are you proud, self-sufficient? Pride will probably manifest itself in some area of your life where you are very good at what you do. I have found that I am the most vulnerable at my point of greatest strength.

What makes pride dangerous is that it leads us to the place where we actually begin to believe we can "get along" without the Lord. Oh, we would never *say* that—not in so many words. But that's how it plays out. "I'm good at this; I can do this well," and we stop praying.

Whenever you see pride raise up its ugly head, let it be a warning to you. See the flashing red lights. Listen to the warning bells. And change course immediately.

God hates pride.[8] He distances himself from the

proud![9] And you never, never want to be on the wrong side of that issue. When the Holy Spirit warns you that you're treading on dangerous ground, listen well!

Remember, Jesus' frustration with the disciples in the garden, the night before his death on the cross?[10] He warned them that they were about to face a difficult time, and that all of them would fail, and walk away from Him. Peter piped in, "Everybody else may fail You, but not me! I will never fail You." Jesus warned him again, but he became even more adamant, "Even if I have to die for you, I will never disown you." Of course, a short time later, as he stood in the courtyard of Caiaphas' house, he denied that he even knew Jesus.

The lesson for us is all too clear: Our time of greatest danger may coincide with at time when we feel the most confidence. As Solomon so aptly phrased it, "Pride goes before destruction, a haughty spirit before a fall" (Proverbs 16:18).

When I was a little boy, my godly mother drilled that Scripture into my head. I was taught to fear pride, and pursue humility.

Just When You Think You Need It Least

Yes, you do need God's help, even when—*especially* when—you think you need it least.

Many years ago I performed the wedding for a couple whose names I will never forget, Dennis and Deanne. It was their BIG day; the day they had planned for, prayed over, and patiently waited for. Their wedding day.

Dennis and I stood on the platform watching, as

Deanne was escorted down the aisle by her father. The congregation stood to their feet, honoring and admiring the beautiful bride. When she arrived at the front, I addressed the bride and groom as Dennis and *Denise*. Remember now, her name is Deanne. I didn't notice, I'm sure everyone else did. Then I prayed over them, once again addressing her as Denise. Why didn't the Lord correct me?

As I began the homily, I said their names once again, and once again I referred to her as Denise, not Deanne. She couldn't take it anymore, and urgently whispered, *"Deanne!"* I apologized, a bit embarrassed, not realizing I had called her by the wrong name three times so far.

I got through the homily unscathed, but then came the vows. I started the vows for the man, by looking at Deanne and saying, "Dennis, would you repeat after me…?" By this time *she* was thoroughly confused, and repeated, "I Dennis, I mean, I Denise…" then stopped in frustration. Of course, everyone in the church was laughing by that point.

A man sitting behind my wife said right out loud, "What is he going to call her next?" I apologized and we finished the ceremony, without error.

Dennis and Denise, I mean Deanne, still attend our church and have fond memories of their wedding day. I however, learned a great lesson that day. Never, ever, get up to speak without asking God for help.

I have preached in the church I pastor over 6,000 times (imagine it!). I know how to speak, and I do okay at it; but I realize that it is only with God's help that what I say will matter in the lives of people.

James had it right when he declared, "God opposes the proud but gives grace to the humble" (James 4:6).

I need that grace. I need *Him*. And so do you.

One day Jesus noticed the guests, at a banquet, choosing to sit in the places of honor. He cautioned the disciples not to choose the highest place, because someone more important than yourself may come in and the host would have to ask you to take a lower place. How humiliating! Then He went on to say that if you take a lower place, perhaps the host will invite you to move to a more prominent place, thereby honoring you."

He concluded, "For everyone who exalts himself will be humbled, and he who humbles himself will be exalted" (Luke 14:11).

Is there any point in your life where you think, "I can do this. I don't need help here"? It very well could be in an area of your greatest strength, doing what you do best and have done a thousand times before.

Be careful! That could be your point of greatest vulnerability.

Could I encourage you to get on your knees and ask God's forgiveness for any point of pride in your life? Kneel every morning before your Commander in Chief, Jesus Christ, and ask for His help to view your life through the eyes of humility, not pride. You'll be glad you did.

And you won't be stuck.

Chapter Four

Don't Get Stuck in Your Thinking

The first winter Ginger and I lived in Montana made us wonder about our decision to move to a winter wonderland. As the months rolled by, the snow seemed to never let up. And since the city didn't have enough snowplows to clear all the side streets, the ruts in front of our house grew deeper and deeper. It became almost impossible to turn out of the well-traveled ruts on the street and pull into my own driveway.

Sometimes our thinking gets in a rut, and it is extremely difficult for us to steer our way into a fresh perspective. More dangerous still, we might not even be aware that we've been stuck...perhaps for a long time. We see something in a particular way, and can't imagine seeing it differently.

Is that dangerous? It depends upon whether our opinions are well-informed, or we are stuck in ignorance. There is a story in the New Testament that addresses the consequences of being stuck in our thinking.[12]

Jesus, and the disciples closest to Him came upon a man who had been blind from birth. And it prompted a question: "Rabbi, who sinned, this man or his parents, that he was born blind?" (John 9:2).

The assumption was that someone had sinned, or he wouldn't be in the condition he was in.

Jesus, however, wasn't stuck in their way of thinking. Essentially, He suggested they stop worrying about who was at fault, and rather ask themselves if there was anything they could do about the man's condition. Then He proceeded to spit on the ground, form some mud with His saliva, put it on the man's eyes, and told the afflicted man to go wash in the Pool of Siloam.

He did, and was immediately healed.

As word got around, the man's acquaintances, of course, were stunned.

His neighbors and those who had formerly seen him begging asked, "Isn't this the same man who used to sit and beg?" Some claimed that he was.

Others said, "No, he only looks like him."

But he himself insisted, "I am the man." (John 9:8-9)

As usual, the Pharisees had to get in the middle of things. These guys had made getting offended into an art form, and they didn't disappoint in this instance. Right out of the box, they condemned the healing because it had been accomplished on the Sabbath.

How could this healing come from God? It didn't conform to their in-house rules.

Imagine coming to the place in your thinking where you would place the observance of a particular day above a man's miraculous healing. They were stuck. There might not have been much snow in Israel, but these guys were locked into ruts a foot deep.

After the man had offended the Pharisees even further by giving credit to Jesus, they kicked him out of the synagogue, effectively ostracizing him from Jewish society.

Jesus, however, pursued the man, and asked, "Do you believe in the Son of Man?"

"Who is he, sir? Tell me so I can believe in him," the man pled. When Jesus made it clear that He was the Son of Man, the man responded immediately, "Lord, I believe," and he worshipped Him.

This man's life was changed forever. Not only was he physically whole, but now, in an instant, he was spiritually transformed.

But then came the kicker, when Jesus revealed an eternal principle concerning this exchange between the Pharisees and the man who had been born blind. "For judgment I have come into this world, so that the blind will see and those who see will become blind."[13] Jesus was saying that there are two kinds of people: those who think they know everything, and are consequently in a rut, stuck in their thinking, and those who are humble enough to recognize they have a lot to learn. The latter group, as a result, are in a position to consistently grow, change, and come to life-stretching discoveries throughout their years.

How *Could* She?

Years ago when we were first married, I distinctly remember when Ginger began to use the word, "Lord."

I knew something was up.

Even though we were Christians, Ginger had vowed never to use that term, because "that's the way the fanatics talked," and we were not fanatics. It was okay to talk about Jesus or God, but "Lord" was a bit over the top.

I became curious about the changes, first in her terminology, and then in behavior. *What's going on with my wife?* I wondered. Finally, I couldn't take it anymore; I just had to say something.

"Ginger, what's going on with you lately?"

She smiled one of those Oh-how-I've-been-hoping-you-would-ask sort of smiles, took a deep breath, and said, "Well, I drove over to the church in Aloha and asked the pastor to pray for me to be filled with the Holy Spirit."

The impact of her words hit me full force. I felt like someone had just knocked the wind out of me. I sat down on the bed, stunned, unable to speak for a moment.

She had violated my command. I had *forbidden* her. I couldn't have made it more clear how dangerous it was to dabble in the things she had now bought into. *How could she?*

The truth is, I was stuck in my thinking.

I could not turn my mental wheels out of the rut in which I had lived through my whole Christian life. I had my adamant beliefs. But what I came to realize over the next several weeks was that my belief system had not been examined in light of Scripture.

Knowing how deeply committed I was to the Scripture, she picked up her Bible, opened to a passage in the book of Acts, handed it to me, and politely requested, "Please read this before you say anything."

I did. Slowly and carefully, I read these words, "When the apostles in Jerusalem heard that Samaria had accepted the word of God, they sent Peter and John to them. When they arrived, they prayed for them that they might receive the Holy Spirit, because the Holy Spirit had not yet come upon any of them; they had simply been baptized into the name of the Lord Jesus. Then Peter and John placed their hands on them, and they received the Holy Spirit."[13]

As I encountered those words, it was as though scales had been removed from my eyes. I didn't know what to say. The passage was clear. These people were believers. They had committed their lives to Christ, had been baptized in water, but the Holy Spirit had not yet come upon them.

This traumatic experience launched me into a study of the Holy Spirit in the New Testament, transforming both my thinking and my experience.

I had been stuck in my thinking. I had not examined my belief in the light of Scripture, and was therefore hindered from moving toward something that would help me become everything God has purposed for me.

I'm sure you have had experiences when you were confronted with a reality you had not faced before. At such times, how would you describe yourself? Are you open to new ideas, willing to examine evidence that may change your thinking, willing to acknowledge when you are wrong?

Or would you rather be…stuck?

As Jesus and the disciples were leaving Jericho, they heard a man call out to Jesus from the back of the crowd. At first, onlookers tried to dissuade the man, but he was so determined that their rebuffs only intensified his efforts. As Bartimaeus continued to cry out, Jesus instructed that he be brought to Him. Filled with hope and anticipation, Bartimaeus leaped to his feet and made his way to Jesus.

Jesus asked him a simple question. "What do you want Me to do for you?"

The blind man's response was straightforward: "I want to see."

I wonder how our thinking might be changed if every day we made that simple request of Jesus: "Lord, today I want to see."

Are you ready for the surprises He probably has in store for you?

Never Stop Asking Questions

In my junior year of high school I took a senior psychology class. Three seats behind me sat Charles, all 155 pounds, and 6 feet 8 inches of him. Charles was not only extraordinarily tall, he had a really big brain (ending up with three PhDs in his college career).

Three doctorates? That wouldn't have surprised anyone in my high school. Charles was the very picture of an eccentric intellectual.

As smart as he was, Charles could still be

extremely exasperating at times. He drove Mr. Hollis bonkers. Every time—and I do mean *every* time—the teacher asked a question, Charles' hand shot up. He had the answer. Always. Even when he didn't have the answer, he had the answer.

This guy always had his hand up. He was inquisitive, curious, questioning, always probing for information, and had a voracious appetite to learn. Such people will never find their mental wheels in a rut.

You may remember that Jesus often taught in parables. He would tell a story, then wait to give the meaning. At that point many people would walk away, never bothering to learn the meaning of what He had just taught. But others would stick around and inquire, "Jesus, I didn't get that. Could you run that by me again?" And He would gladly explain further.[14]

Here's my simple counsel: Don't ever come to the place where you think you know everything. Keep asking questions, search, probe, dig, and inquire, until you finally get to the truth.

Wait Before You Speak

The apostle James provides another important clue for avoiding mental ruts:

> My dear brothers, take note of this: Everyone should be quick to listen, slow to speak and slow to become angry. (James 1:19)

Solomon put it this way:

He who answers before listening—
that is his folly and his shame.
(Proverbs 18:13)

My mother had her own way of getting that point across. "Stan," she would say, "you have two ears and one mouth. Use them accordingly."

In any listing of courses in high school or college, you can usually find plenty of speech classes. But how many classes have you taken about how to listen? So much learning takes place when we simply follow the biblical mandate, "be quick to listen, and slow to speak."

My youngest daughter Kelly and her husband Tim lived with Ginger and me for a few months. Joey, the parrot, was part of the package. Tim, an avid Denver Broncos fan, had taught Joey how to say, "Go Broncos."

In order to torment my son-in-law, I decided to teach Joey how to say, "Go Vikings." Because Joey's cage was in a prominent place in our home, I passed by our feathered guest multiple times every day. And every time I did, I leaned close to Joey and said, "Go Vikings!"

Poor Joey became very confused. In a few weeks he was forcefully saying, "Go Vikos!" Actually, he picked up more than I intended. He would say, "Go Vikos! Hee, hee, hee!" He had even picked up my chuckle.

Anyone can repeat verbiage. But if we want to speak intelligently, we must learn from others. Listening is a learned art, and must be practiced. But once learned, you can't even imagine what an advantage it gives us.

As it says in the book of Proverbs: *"Even a fool is thought wise if he keeps silent."* [15]

Invite the Input of Others

A number of years ago I went skiing for the first time. My instructor was a close personal friend, who also happened to be an exceptional skier. He took me up in the lift, seemingly halfway up the mountain, and we stood together before the ski run he had selected.

I looked down that hill, and it was plenty steep. My stomach constricted under my layers of warm clothing. *What in the world am I doing here?* I asked myself. I was so frightened I felt like I couldn't even move a muscle, let alone attempt to ski down that plunging slope.

My friend however, flashed a big smile, and assured me that everything was under control. I could manage this, no problem. As we proceeded down the hill, he skied backwards, in front of me, coaching me as we traversed the hill. Downhill from someone like me? That seemed just a little foolish!

We hadn't gone too far when he said to me, "Stan, I want you to put your weight on the downhill ski."

What? I thought to myself. That seemed completely counterintuitive. If anything it felt like I should do the opposite, leaning into the hill. But thanks to the input of a good friend, I managed to ski all the way down the hill. And I did it again and again, gaining more confidence (and having more fun) each time.

Finally, I achieved the ultimate: skiing all the way down the hill without falling a single time. Proud of my accomplishment, I headed for the area around the picnic tables where my friends were enjoying lunch. When I came to a stop, even I was impressed. I announced, so that everyone within fifty yards could hear, "Hey, I made it all the way down the hill without falling!" At that very instant my skis went out from under me and I was immediately on my back. Where was my friend when I needed him?

Have you ever gone to someone for advice—perhaps a teacher, parent, pastor, or close friend—and came away with a lustrous pearl of knowledge that made all the difference in your thinking? Have you ever been in an argument, and suddenly realized you were wrong and your opponent was right? You can learn from friends who disagree with you, as well as those who agree.

What a great way to get unstuck in your thinking…with input from a trusted friend.

Never Stop Reading

How many books did you read last year? People who read widely will not get stuck in their thinking. In fact, it's quite the opposite; they will be learning, growing, constantly seeing things in a different, and helpful way.

One of my practices is to occasionally ask my friends, "What are the best three books you have read this year?" or "What are you reading these days?" I'm always interested in knowing what books others would recommend. After all, each of us only has a limited time in which we can read. I don't know about you, but I want to invest that time wisely!

You know what it's like, don't you, to be reading a good book, and suddenly come upon something that grabs your attention? You reach for a pen and underline it, reading it again, more slowly this time. Sometimes when I do that, I turn back to the front of the book, find a blank page, and write down the page number and a memory jogger, so I don't lose that important information.

The average reader reads about twenty five pages an hour. If you devote one hour a day to reading, you can read the average book in about ten days. In other words, you can read over thirty books a year, without an inordinate investment of time.

One of my granddaughters is an avid reader. Everyone else may be standing around visiting, doing pretty much nothing, while she's in the other room, deeply engrossed in a good book. She will never get stuck in her thinking!

If you're already a reader, how about varying your diet from time to time? If you only read contemporary fiction, try a classic from another generation. If you only read Bible study books, change up your routine a little and read a travelogue, or a book of humor, or maybe *The Chronicles of Narnia*. The key is to keep your mind stimulated, and keep learning as you're turning the pages.

Don't Be So Sure of Everything

One evening our family was seated around the dinner

table when my youngest daughter, Kelly, announced that she had learned something new in kindergarten that day.

"What did you learn, Kelly?" I asked her.

"A tomato," she informed us, "is a fruit."

I smiled. How cute. "No, honey," I assured her. "Tomatoes are vegetables." Didn't everyone know that?

She appealed to me. "But Daddy, my teacher said—"

I cut her off sharply. "Well, your teacher doesn't know what she's talking about. A tomato is a vegetable."

After all, I'd had a lot of experience with such things. I was well informed. Hadn't I worked in the grocery business for a number of years? Think about it. You go to the produce aisle and what do you see? You see green onions, radishes, lettuce, and, tomatoes—all of those veggies, right there together.

Kelly, bless her heart, continued to defend her newly-minted knowledge, even against such a confident counterattack.

I could see there was only way to settle this argument. I got up, grabbed a dictionary from the bookshelf, brought it back to the table, and smugly prepared to set my little daughter to rights. Never mind that I was arguing with a five year old, I was anxious to prove my point. After all, my fatherly knowledge and authority were at issue here.

Trouble was, Kelly and her teacher were right.

Tomatoes are, and presumably always have been, part of the fruit family. There it was, and I couldn't argue with it. I had been so sure…but so wrong!

The truth is, defensiveness is often a clear signal of being stuck in your opinions. But think about it: If you're so sure of yourself and so supremely confident, why do you get defensive when you're challenged?

Next time you find yourself bristling over something, you might ask yourself, "*What's going on here? Why am I so uptight about this?*" The fact is, we're usually defensive because we believe something, but don't know how to defend our belief. If we would investigate a bit further, we might discover that we've been stuck.

You can feel bad about the guy who's stuck in the mud and gets out of his car to survey the situation. But that, at least, is step one to getting unstuck. He'll figure something out. He'll call his insurance company, he'll call 9-1-1, or he'll call his brother-in-law with the pickup. Save your pity for the guy who's been stuck in the mud for years, going nowhere…and doesn't even realize it.

Chapter Five

Don't Get Stuck on the World

Ginger got on the phone with her friend, Mary, and after one cheery hello, didn't say another word for a few minutes.

Then suddenly, my wife broke into a fit of laughter.

As it turns out, Mary had been busy around the house that morning, then suddenly remembered she had forgotten to take her prescription. Reaching for the bottle in the medicine chest, she shook out two pills, washed them down with a glass of water, and went on her way.

Suddenly, the horrible realization hit her that she had opened the wrong bottle…and had just swallowed two quite strong sleeping pills.

There she was, facing a busy morning, wondering, *What in the world am I going to do now?* She quickly picked up the phone to call her daughter Nancy, hoping to receive some advice. Or at least a little sympathy.

Nancy, however, was no help at all.

"Night-night, Mommy," she said cheerfully.

After the laughter calmed down, Nancy did submit a couple of options. "Mom, you could go the store and get some Red Bull—or go to City Brew and get a four-shot espresso. But you'd better hurry."

Mary had a full day before her, and we know what that's like, don't we? We pack our days with the stuff of life—family, work, school, church, friendships, and hopefully some fun squeezed in. Most of us can't afford to be distracted or less than on top of our game. And Mary certainly didn't want to wind down before she even got wound up.

Jesus also had a friend named Mary. In her several New Testament appearances, she always seems to be at the feet of Jesus. In Luke 10, we see her contrasted to her sister, Martha. Martha also loved the Lord with all her heart, but when He visited their home, she became so busy waiting on Jesus that she failed to sit down and spend quality time with Him.

I once heard Bill Hybels say, "The pace at which I was doing the work of God was destroying the work of God in me." That describes Martha. She was serving Jesus with a loving heart, but her service was taking her away from *being* with Jesus.

One of the words used in this text to describe Martha is translated into English as "upset."[16] After doing a deeper study of this term, I discovered it communicates the idea of being turbid.

Let me explain. Once I picked up a jar of what appeared to be clear water. Unknown to me, there were sediments that had settled to the bottom of the jar, so when I shook it, the water became murky, or turbid.

That's how Jesus described Martha. Turbid,

cloudy, murky. Her life was so filled with activity, she could no longer see things clearly.

Most of us, I suspect, have been there, our lives so caught up in the pressures and flurry of living that we lose sight of appropriate priorities. So often it seems, in the midst of all the activity, Jesus is slowly eased to the perimeter of our lives. We're lulled to sleep, spiritually, and become vulnerable to the innumerable entice-ments of the world, that can so quickly draw us into sin.

So, take note…the sheer busyness of life, simply allowing ourselves to be overwhelmed with activity, is one of the ways we can get stuck, focusing only on the world.

Watch Out!

Another way to get stuck on the world is through greed. Jesus gave us a very strong warning about that danger.

"Watch out! Be on your guard against all kinds of greed; a man's life does not consist in the abundance of his possessions." [17]

We've all had to wrestle with that particular incli-nation at one time or another. Without really intend-ing to, we find ourselves drawn in by our desire for certain physical possessions…a new home, furniture, a boat, a motorcycle. Allowing ourselves to follow this Pied Piper of materialism, we stumble into the mud-hole of self-indulgence. And we get stuck on the world, stuck in sin, where we really don't want to be. When we violate the guidelines God has placed on our lives, we normally do so in the name of finding freedom, just as Adam and Eve did. But we end up (like them) enticed away from a healthy relationship to God, and dragged into bondage.[18]

If not dealt with quickly and appropriately, sin gets a grip on our lives, controlling our thoughts and actions. With our wheels uselessly spinning in this marshy, unhappy place, we end up living a life far less than God's high purpose for us.

Allow me to put forth some suggestions on how you might avoid becoming stuck on the world.

Focus on the Presence of Jesus

For most of my adult life, I have gotten up early each morning to begin my day alone with Jesus. I have found this to be one of the most effective ways to keep Jesus at the center of my life.

Occasionally I talk to someone about this important issue and they'll tell me, "You know, right now I'm just too busy."

I used to fall for that one, thinking, *Well, maybe they really are too busy.* And then Elizabeth told me her story, and I revised my opinion of the "too busy" excuse.

Due to circumstances outside her control, Elizabeth lived a very full and hectic life. I knew she worked full-time, had several children, and was married to an alcoholic who was often at home. So I was a bit skeptical when she began telling me all the things the Lord had been showing her.

"Elizabeth," I asked her, "when did the Lord show you all these things? I know what a busy life you lead."

She bowed her head. "Well, Pastor," she said quietly, "because my life is so chaotic, every afternoon, when I put the kids down for a nap, I get my Bible and prayer journal, and go into the bathroom, lock the door, sit down on the floor and read my Bible and pray. That seems to be the only time I can get alone to be with Jesus."

Tears filled my eyes. I was silent, unable to speak for a few moments, stunned by the dedication of this, sweet, godly woman. Elizabeth made a mark on my life that day, taking away all the excuses for not taking time to be with Jesus regularly.

Be on Your Guard for the Deceitfulness of Wealth

Jesus told a story we have come to know as the Parable of the Sower. In that story, Jesus tells us how some of the good seed took root in the soil, only to be choked by weeds and thorns. He went on to describe these thorns as "the worries of this life and the deceitfulness of wealth."[19]

Think about that expression: *the deceitfulness of wealth.* We live in a world that measures a person's worth on the basis of how much money he makes, or how many possessions she is able to accumulate. I haven't ever met a follower of Christ who would admit it, but so many of us live that way.

Apparently, we believe the promise of our world—that joy and fulfillment come through wealth and the accumulation of stuff. Jesus calls this kind of thinking a deception.[20]

Fascinated by this term "deceitfulness," I looked up "deceit" in the dictionary and discovered that it means "failure to fulfill a promise."[21] We will find ourselves deeply disappointed if we believe wealth and possessions will bring fulfillment and joy into our lives. The pursuit of happiness through possessions will invariably lead us away from a life focused on Jesus.

Refocus on Jesus

A man came to Jesus, asking how he might find eternal life.[22] Eternal life can refer to *quantity* of life, living forever in heaven, or a *quality* of life, including fulfillment in the here-and-now. We know by the conversation that follows that in this case, eternal life refers to the latter.

Jesus responded to the young man's question by instructing him to obey God's commandments. The young man shot back that he had obeyed God's commandments all of his life, but still remained unfulfilled. Jesus then offered a startling suggestion: "If you want to be perfect, go, sell your possessions and give to the poor, and you will have treasure in heaven. Then come, follow me."[23]

The young man must have thought to himself, *Are you crazy? Cash out all my investments and drop it in a Salvation Army kettle? You've got to be kidding!*

The Scripture records his response succinctly: "He went away sad, because he had great wealth."[24]

He sought Jesus' advice, but ignored it. And so he left as he had come...focused on the world, unfulfilled, stuck. As Jesus and His disciples dialogued about this incident, Peter piped in, "We have left everything to follow you! What then will there be for us?"[25]

If only the rich young man would have asked that question, how different his life would have been! Jesus addressed the very thing the young man (and so many of us) fear: *If I follow Jesus, I'll get ripped off. I'll miss out on life.* The truth is quite the opposite. Notice Jesus' response to Peter's question.

"And everyone who has left houses or brothers or sisters or father or mother or fields for my sake will receive a hundred times as much and will inherit eternal life."[26]

When I think about that statement, I must ask myself, "Would I trade my life now, as a follower of Christ, for my life before I submitted myself to Him?"

It doesn't take a great deal of thought to answer that question, *Not in a million years!* I have never entertained such a thought, nor have I talked to a sincere Christ-follower who has. Why would we trade our life in Jesus—forgiveness, freedom, confidence, and peace—for a life of confusion, fear, and shame?

Recognizing how much better off we are having made the decision to follow Jesus, let's remain resolute to keep our eyes focused on Him.

Understand God's Provision

Recently, I entered the world that every man fantasizes about…the world of motorcycles.

It took an enormous amount of pleading, begging, groveling, even manipulating, but finally Ginger relented. Even so, she remained *very* concerned for my safety. Searching the web, she came across a site featuring an expert who trains motorcycle policemen, the top two percent of bike riders in America. Unbeknownst to me, she sent an e-mail to this man, expressing her gnawing concerns about me learning to ride a bike at my age, with no previous experience. He quickly wrote back, affirming the validity of her concerns, but thankfully, offered a solution. He pointed her to a couple of DVDs, which I eventually purchased.

I learned many valuable lessons from his instruction, but I also learned a great spiritual lesson I'm sure he had no intention of teaching. Here it is: "You will go where you look, so look where you want to go."

Over and over again he pointed out, "If you want to turn left, look left. If you want to turn right, look right. Under no circumstances look down, or you will go down!"

This is great spiritual advice as well. *You will go where you look, so look where you want to go.*

If your life is focused on materialism, you'll end up being a materialistic person. If you're focused on possessions, making money, amassing things for yourself, you'll end up bound by greed. If you enter the world of pornography, your mind will become so consumed that you will end up acting out the dark and terrible things you have seen. If your mind is filled with lust for someone other than your spouse, you will end up living out that reality.

Jesus, the greatest teacher of all time, taught us this same truth: "Do not store up for yourselves treasures on earth, where moth and rust destroy, and where thieves break in and steal. But store up for yourselves treasures in heaven, where moth and rust do not destroy, and where thieves do not break in and steal. *For where your treasure is, there your heart will be also."* [27]

He encouraged us to not allow ourselves to live lives focused on possessions and materialism, then went on to tell us we instead should live in the reality of God's commitment to provide for us.[28]

Until you come to live in the confidence and assurance of God's great provision, you will not only focus unduly on possessions, but you will worry about your needs being met.

Worry is counterproductive, consuming our thoughts and drawing us away from a healthy productive life. You've heard the old expression about a dog "worrying a bone." It's another way of describing the way he keeps biting and gnawing and chewing on that thing until he's worn it down to a nub. That's what happens when our minds "worry" on some issue. We expend our limited supply of mental and emotional energy turning something around and around in our minds, when we ought to be laying it at the Lord's feet, and letting *Him* deal with it.

Simplify

As frustrated as we may feel with our overcrowded lives at times, we may feel that there's little we can do about it. We tell ourselves, *Well, that's just the way it is.*

Are we surrendering too quickly to the way of life the world attempts to foist upon us? Are we really at the mercy of circumstances?

I love the word *responsibility*, which of course communicates "response ability." God created us with the ability and freedom to choose how we will live our lives. Sometimes we forget, and give in to thoughts like these: "Well, I'm Irish. We Irish have bad tempers, you know." Or maybe, "This is what my mom and dad ingrained in me all my life. It's just the way I am." Or we may play the victim card, shrugging our shoulders and saying, "I guess I'm at the mercy of my situation."

That kind of thinking, real as it may seem to us, is not reality. We *are* free to choose how we will live our lives. We are "response–able."

Are you stuck on the world, stuck in its way of thinking? Have you given in to the pressure to focus on possessions? Have you invested in the world's measure of success? Have you allowed yourself to get caught up in the hectic lifestyle that dominates our culture, the high-speed treadmill that leads to nowhere? Have you allowed the world to impose its distorted sense of morality on you? You can do something about it!

You're only as stuck as you think you are.

Unstuck at a Price

I was looking over my appointment book one morning, and saw her name.

I thought to myself, *Why in the world would she be coming to see me?* I was a bit concerned because she had left our church causing hurt, confusion, and deeply strained relationships. Frankly, I had never expected to see her again.

When she left, intent on divorcing her husband, we pled, counseled, and did everything within our power to discourage her from walking away from her marriage. But she had allowed herself to be enticed into an immoral relationship.

Now, several years later, her name was in my appointment book. I was curious, but just a bit unnerved.

Finally, the time arrived for her appointment. My assistant opened my office door, allowing the woman in, then shut the door, turned, and walked back to her office. I stood, ready to greet the woman, but before I could, she fell on her knees on the floor and began weeping and pleading, in intense agony.

"Please forgive me, please forgive me, oh Jesus, please forgive me for what I have done," she begged. "Oh, Pastor Stan, can you ever forgive me for what I've done to you and to the church?"

I slowly got down on my knees, in front of her. I can't remember being more humbled. I then reached out my hand, placing it on her shoulder, and quietly said, "Oh yes, I can forgive you, and I do."

We spent the next few minutes praying together. First I prayed, and then she called out to God, opening her broken and repentant heart to Him.

I can't remember in all my years of leading a church a more sincere, emotional, and heartfelt plea for forgiveness. Here was a young woman who fell prey to temptation, got caught in the snare of the god of this world, and lived out the consequences, stuck in the misery of her sin. But thank God, she came to the reality of what she had done, and was set free.

Do you recognize any place in your life where you have taken your eyes off of Jesus and begun to focus on an enticement of this world? Remember, you will go where you look, so look where you want to go.

Chapter Six

Don't Get Stuck in the Book

Uncle Eddie never went anywhere without a book.

Family reunions would come around, and the rest of us would be outside enjoying the sunshine and the company of people we loved.

Not Uncle Eddie.

He was in the house reading anything and everything he could get his hands on. On several occasions, I saw him grab an encyclopedia and read for hours, like most people would read a novel.

But here's the thing about Uncle Eddie: he might have been regarded as a little eccentric or antisocial by the family from time to time, but he didn't live with his head in the clouds. Although endlessly hungry for knowledge, Uncle Eddie didn't spend *all* his time in books. In fact, much that he learned he put into practice. He wrote a college calculus textbook. On another occasion, he *completely* disassembled his classic 1949 Cadillac. There were engine parts all over the workbench in his garage. He tore that Cadillac down to a mass of parts, then put it back together again. It ran like a clock, both before and after he worked on it.

The classic bookworm, I suppose, is best known for having a nose buried in a book. For Uncle Eddie, however, that was a means to an end. What impressed me was that he took his knowledge *and put it to use.*

A few months after I committed my life to Christ, I pretty much became a bookworm, too.

With my Bible.

I couldn't seem to get enough time in the Scriptures. I, too, was hungry for knowledge. I spent hours in the college library, devouring my *Good News For Modern Man New Testament* when I should have been studying for my classes. In a few months, my New Testament looked like a family heirloom—pages worn, cover tattered, and every page marked with notes and highlights.

It's important for you to know, because of the topic at hand, that I have loved the Bible and respected it as God's Word all of my life.

When I first showed interest in following Christ, our pastor gave me a little New Testament I still have today. At the age of five, I was preaching fervently. I couldn't read yet, but wow, could I preach! I would place my Testament on a little gray stool, open it to who knows where, and then rip loose with a hellfire and brimstone sermon. I was pretty good.

Even during my rebellious years, I respected the Scriptures. I always had a Bible sitting in a prominent place in the living room—even though I never read it. Looking at it and having it around was one thing; reading it was just too uncomfortable in that season of my life.

It was the Word of God that brought me to the point of salvation, and once there, I became hungry to know it, eventually devoting myself to teaching the Scriptures as a vocation.

To this day the Bible is an inseparable part of my daily life. It is where I turn for words of comfort …where I search for answers to the complex problems of life…and where I turn when I need guidance. It corrects me, encourages me, gives me security, and gives me confidence in a complex world.

The apostle Paul declares that the Scriptures are "God breathed," or inspired by God (2 Timothy 3:16). The Bible teaches us what is right, what is not right, how to get right, and how to stay right.[29]

Why do I go into so much detail when I say that I love and revere the Bible? Because I want you to understand something: When I say, "Don't get stuck in the book," I don't mean value it less, study it less, or memorize it less.

I do mean, obey it more.

I do mean, put it into practice.

Like my Uncle Eddie, we want to be people who study thoroughly, but then do something with what we've learned.

A Glance in the Mirror?

The apostle James gave us the following advice:

> Do not merely listen to the word, and so deceive yourselves. Do what it says. Anyone

who listens to the word but does not do what it says is like a man who looks at his face in a mirror and, after looking at himself, goes away and immediately forgets what he looks like. But the man who looks intently into the perfect law that gives freedom, and continues to do this, not forgetting what he has heard, but doing it—he will be blessed in what he does. (James 1:22-25)

Ladies, can you imagine walking up to a mirror first thing in the morning, taking a good look at yourself, and then walking away without doing anything about what you saw? Unthinkable! You immediately reach for the hairbrush, then the toothbrush, then hurriedly put on some makeup before you even consider being seen by anyone.

Guys, you wouldn't walk up to a mirror, see spinach in your teeth, and walk away doing nothing about it. You'd do something about it, pronto.

James makes it clear that the Word of God actually reveals to us what we look like. Not just on the surface, but deep down where no other eyes can see. Scripture lays bare our weaknesses and points out character flaws, potential danger signs, and sins. It would be foolish to walk away from it without correcting what we see. James encourages us to hear the truth of God's Word, and then do something about it. And further promises we will be blessed if we do.

All my life, I have been around followers of Christ who pride themselves in knowing God's Word. They're hungry for knowledge. Churches are known for their teaching, pastors for their impeccable theology, and congregants for their knowledge of Scripture. I'm simply suggesting that when we get to heaven, the Lord isn't going to give us a pop quiz on how much Scripture we know, but He is going to talk to us about our willingness to do what He asked of us.

Live By It

You believe the Bible. Do you live by its truths? Does this Book influence your daily life, or have you compartmentalized it, safely divided and separated from your real moment-by-moment life on this planet?

Let's do a little exercise to see how much this book impacts our lives. Read the Scriptures below and answer the questions that follow.

> "Give, and it will be given to you. A good measure, pressed down, shaken together and running over, will be poured into your lap. For with the measure you use, it will be measured to you." (Luke 6:38)

Please notice the promise of that verse. If you are a generous person, it will come back to you, multiplied. *Do you believe that?* If you do, your belief will affect your behavior. Your giving practices will be impacted. Are you a generous giver—toward your church, the poor, and mission efforts around the world?

> Each one of you also must love his wife as he loves himself, and the wife must respect her

husband. (Ephesians 5:33)

Does the Bible influence how you treat your spouse? Do you treat your wife with Christ's love? Did you do so last night? Did you practice that this morning? And wives, do you truly show respect to your husbands?

Fathers, do not exasperate your children; instead, bring them up in the training and instruction of the Lord. (Ephesians 6:4)

Would your children say the Bible has affected how you relate to them? Do you frustrate them or speak words of fulfillment to them? Are you instructing them in the ways of the Lord and providing a positive example for them of a healthy and committed Christ follower?

Whatever you do, work at it with all your heart, as working for the Lord, not for men. (Colossians 3:23)

Do people at work respect you for your diligence in the workplace? Are you exemplary in your lifestyle? Do they respect you for your faith?

But among you there must not be even a hint of sexual immorality, or of any kind of impurity, or of greed, because these are improper for God's holy people. (Ephesians 5:3)

Has the Bible influenced your behavior in terms of morality? Are you pure sexually? Do you have a handle on greed?

In other words, you believe this book is true; do you live like it?

Expect to be Stretched

Over thirty years of pastoral ministry have shown me…if you believe the Book and make a decision to live by it, you will experience huge challenges to your faith. He will lead you through experiences that will stretch your limits.

A number of years ago, I settled into a first-class aisle seat and prepared for a long flight home. (Don't you just love upgrades?) The plane had been pushed back from the gate, but now we didn't seem to be going anywhere.

I could hear the conversation between the pilot and co-pilot, methodically going through their pre-flight checklist. Finally, I heard the engineer say, "We just lost our first generator."

I thought, *This can't be good.* At that moment, I knew what no other passenger on that plane knew. We weren't going anywhere.

I turned to the guy sitting next to me, to fill him in. He wasn't happy. "Oh, great," he said, with obvious frustration. "I don't want to spend the night here."

As our waiting continued, I got out my Bible and notebook and began to review a sermon I'd been working on. The subject line stared up at me from a sheet of notebook paper: *The importance of sharing our faith.*

The man sitting next to me was working on what appeared to be a manuscript.

"Are you an editor?" I asked.

"No," he said quietly, glancing my way. "I'm a movie producer."

I glanced back at my message. I felt pretty confident that I'd identified all the right Bible passages. I had a good handle on my four points, closing illustration, and final appeal.

It was a good message. But was I willing to live it…*right then?* Would I seek to open a conversation with this big-time Hollywood guy, and (somehow) bring the element of my faith to the table? Would he sneer at a Foursquare pastor from Montana?

Suddenly, the plane began to move again. Apparently we didn't need our first generator.

Keying off his words about being a movie producer, I breathed a quick prayer and plunged in.

"Well, I guess you and I are in the same boat," I said. "We're both in the business of influencing people."

He looked my way, probably not wanting to acknowledge he was in the same business as a pastor. But then he said, "It's a big responsibility, isn't it?"

As we conversed, sporadically, over the next couple of hours, there were several junctures at which I had to decide, *Will I keep pursuing this conversation? Will I take the initiative to talk about Jesus? Am I willing to take the heat from this guy, and face his rejection?*

Obviously, God was putting me to the test. Was this something I just talk about, and ask others to do, or was I willing to put it into practice? Here was my opportunity sitting right beside me. *Lord, please just open the door.*

A Holy-Spirit boldness came over me, and I suddenly blurted, "Please forgive me for bothering you."

"No problem," he said. "Please go ahead. I don't mind."

So I went on. "They used to make a lot of movies based on Bible stories, but they don't seem to do that much anymore. Why is that? Does it reflect a cultural shift away from Christianity?"

He responded immediately. "No, actually it's very simple. If a producer thinks it would be profitable to make a movie like that, he would do it. It's about money. That's the bottom line."

I sat for a few moments. He was now looking out the window at flashes of lightning. *Appropriate,* I thought. *Flashes of lightning while we're talking about God.*

Then I continued to probe, "So how big a demographic would it take to make it profitable?"

"Well, it depends on how much money you want to invest in the movie. If you're willing to spend big money, you'd better have a big demographic."

So I threw a few stats at him about the number of people in America who believe in God, and the percentage of people who say they are born-again Christians. He didn't blink.

Then I said, "If I were a movie producer, I would think that would be a pretty big audience. In fact, look what CBS has done on Sunday night with the show, 'Touched By An Angel.' I have also noticed how many movies they air on Sunday night that are appropriate for kids and are Christian-friendly. CBS must have made a decision about an important market they could target."

He looked at me very seriously, and said, "You probably won't like this, but I am producing a show that is about to replace 'Touched By An Angel' on Sunday night."

Really? I thought to myself. Now I was really impressed with this guy.

Then came my final ploy, I said, "Are you familiar with the story of Joseph, in the Old Testament?"

"Of course," he responded.

"Why don't you make a movie about Joseph? There is betrayal, temptation, overcoming in the midst of adversity, and a dream come true. It's all there!"

He nodded his head, and said, "It is a great story, isn't it?"

Well, I haven't seen a movie come out recently on Joseph, but you never know. When I got off the plane, he was standing on the ramp, waiting for his friend. As I walked by, I smiled and said, "Nice visiting with you."

He looked at me, and said cheerfully, "I very much enjoyed talking with you."

I have no idea if my conversation impacted this man or not. I didn't lead him to Christ, but I'm convinced I gave him an opportunity to take a step or two in the right direction. The rest of the evening, I was exhilarated by this conversation and thankful I had obeyed the prompting of the Holy Spirit to put into practice what I know.

Isn't that exactly what James said?

But if you look carefully into the perfect law

that sets you free, and if you do what it says and don't forget what you heard, *then God will bless you for doing it.* (1:25, NLT)

Another translation says, "That person will find delight and affirmation in the action." (THE MESSAGE)

There is something about reading the Bible, thinking about its truths, and then finding a way to put those truths to work that floods the soul with *delight.* Why is that? Because we've taken truth out of the realm of the theoretical and woven it through the fabric of our real life…and we see that it works! It's real. What an affirmation!

Imagine that for years you maintained a beautiful set of tools out in a shiny red cabinet in your garage. In your collection, let's say that you had every size of screw driver, every cordless power tool imaginable, and dozens of wrenches right off the hardware store shelf, gleaming in their newness. But how satisfying would it be to arrange and polish those tools every night—but never actually use them? Can you imagine how fun it would be if your wife asked you to do a handyman job and you picked up some of those shiny tools and actually did something with them? What a feeling of satisfaction!

Tools were made to use, not polish. And Scripture was made by God to not only declare truth, but to change lives.

Shelter in the Storm

Every one of us gets to make a decision about God's

Word. If we choose to keep our Bible knowledge in the realm of theory, separating it from the way we really live and respond to life situations, what we're really saying is that we know more than God does. Or think that we can better order and guide our own lives than He can.

What an absurd thought.

The Bible not only promises a blessing and delight for those who put its truths to work, but Jesus Himself promises that we'll experience a stability and steadiness in our lives beyond anything we've experienced before. Consider what He said as He was wrapping up the Sermon on the Mount.

> "Therefore everyone who hears these words of mine and puts them into practice is like a wise man who built his house on the rock. The rain came down, the streams rose, and the winds blew and beat against that house; yet it did not fall, because it had its foundation on the rock." (Matthew 7:24-25)

The storms of life are inevitable, and yet, for those who faithfully respond to God's Word in their daily lives, there will be stability.

We will withstand the storms.

Chapter Seven

Don't Get Stuck in an Experience

Desiring to bring a bit of levity to a serious topic, I once gave a talk from Acts chapter two, while holding a cow tongue. You can imagine the initial response of the congregation: shock, disgust, groans, and gasps filled the room.

That cow tongue was gross (particularly by the end of the third Sunday morning service). But it also communicated my recognition that for many people, my topic of discussion that morning wasn't particularly pleasant.

Tongues.

What comes to mind when you see that word? Fear, dread, uncertainty, delight, wonder, beauty, the Holy Spirit, Pentecost? Insert your own word.

All that to say, I realize this issue of speaking in tongues—praying in the Spirit, or a prayer language—is a sensitive and potentially divisive issue for many followers of Christ. It seems that in recent years, however, there has been more tolerance and acceptance of this practice throughout the Body of Christ.

I was brought up with a very negative point of view on this topic, though I was fairly ignorant about what the Bible really had to say about it.

My wife, Ginger, only attended church sporadically during her childhood, but has a vivid memory of a Sunday evening service at a small Pentecostal church. At one point during the service, a lady sitting directly behind Ginger stood up and started screaming in tongues. Ginger and her brother froze, looking at each other in alarm, wondering what in the world was happening.

Then the woman, completely oblivious to what she was doing, began hitting Ginger on the head with her Bible, as she continued to scream. Ginger put her arms over her head to protect herself, as she and her brother laughed hysterically. You might say that it wasn't an experience that endeared either of them to speaking in tongues.

With that backdrop, imagine my shock when Ginger brought home the book, *They Speak With Other Tongues*, by John Sherrill. I flipped out! I was terrified that my wife would have such a book in the house.

I warned her, "Ginger, stay away from that stuff! Those people are crazy. They work themselves up into a frenzy. It's awful!" To be honest, however, I had very little firsthand experience to validate my opinion.

Thankfully, Ginger wasn't put off by my dire warnings. In fact, she became more and more curious, reading John Sherrill's book to find out if her husband had been correct in his assumptions.

As you may remember from a previous chapter,

Ginger's curiosity and resulting experiences eventually drove me to begin to search the Scriptures for myself. I wanted to determine, as best I could, what the Bible actually has to say on this subject.

I've already chronicled the fear and skepticism I experienced after discovering that Ginger had prayed to be baptized with the Holy Spirit, and to speak in a new language. Just three weeks later, however, after my own extensive search of the Scriptures, I began to ask Jesus to fill me with the Holy Spirit.

I went to bed one night frustrated and puzzled, because Jesus didn't seem to be answering my prayer. I remember clearly burying my face in my pillow, and crying out to Him once again, "Jesus, I believe this is for today, and it's for me. Please baptize me with the Holy Spirit."

After praying for a few moments, I chose to begin speaking, but not in English, the only language I had learned. What came out of my mouth didn't seem like much of a language at the time, but it reminded me of the Iranian students who hung out in the student union, at the college I attended. I was speaking this strange language, and grinning from ear to ear, aware that Jesus had answered my prayer.

After a few minutes, I paused, jumped out of bed and ran into the dining room, where Ginger was working at the table. It was immediately obvious to her that something had happened. I told her what had taken place, then ran back into the bedroom, where I began to speak again.

Now, fast-forward the tape thirty-five years. I am still using my prayer language almost every day, and it is a meaningful part of my spiritual walk.

I have come to believe, confirmed by my experience, that the baptism with the Holy Spirit and speaking in a new language are for today, and are very helpful in our walk with Christ. Biblically, the fullness of the Holy Spirit facilitates our transformation into the image of Christ, making it possible for us to accomplish the primary task for which He has called us: to bring other men, women, and children into relationship with Him.

Speaking in a prayer language is a wonderful experience.

I'm just saying, don't get stuck there.

Instead, allow the experience to propel you toward what Jesus desires: your personal transformation, so you can impact others to follow Christ. He wants to change us, so we can change the world.

Stalled in an Experience

I'm confident that the Lord never intended this experience of a new prayer language to be some kind of a "spiritual badge," somehow making us more significant than others. Nor did He intend it as an experience that we could point back to and say, "I've got it!" Instead, *He is interested in what this experience leads us toward, and helps us accomplish.* And He intends that we *continue* to walk in the fullness of the Holy Spirit. Ephesians 5:18b could read, "…be being filled with the Spirit."

Over thirty years ago, my friend Jim began talking to me in an excited voice about a church he had attended the night before. He said, "They're meeting again tonight. Would you like to go with me?"

He had told me just enough about the service to make me nervous. I'm the conservative type when it comes to the exuberant and the unexpected in church. But Jim assured me he would let me know before the really strange stuff started, so we could slip out quietly. This only served to make me more apprehensive, but I agreed to go.

Once.

And as it turned out, once was plenty.

We walked into the small, simply-decorated room. A drum set occupied one corner of the room, and there was a small platform up front, with one chair off to one side. A few early arrivers mingled, happily talking to each other.

A few minutes later, someone stepped onto the platform and asked us to stand. The music was lively, but unfamiliar, so I had a difficult time participating. At one point during the worship, a man entered from behind the platform and stood behind the person leading. I correctly assumed he was the pastor.

We sang several songs, sat down, then the pastor stood to speak, for ten or fifteen minutes. It didn't seem to me that he had spent a great deal of time in preparation, but the message was mercifully brief. I once heard someone say, "I've never heard a sermon I didn't get something out of, but I've had a few close calls." This was definitely a close call for me.

At the conclusion of the message, he began to pray, loudly, and others in the small congregation joined in with him. As time went on, the volume continued to increase. Up to this point, my anxiety had proven unwarranted. But that was soon to change.

I heard someone stirring directly behind me. It's difficult to describe adequately what came next, but a woman started hissing and moaning, again and again. It seemed as though she was coming closer and closer to the back of my head, where goose bumps were now appearing. Chills were surging up and down my back.

My eyes flew open, and my head jerked toward my friend, who was smiling sympathetically in my direction. "I think we should go now," he said. I was ecstatic, and quite relieved, as we moved hurriedly toward the back door.

Thirty years later, that night is still branded in my brain. Here is the interesting thing to me as I look back. Those same few people gathered every night of the week, with the exception of Monday, and did basically the same thing, week after week, year after year. From my perspective, they were stuck!

They never got beyond their experience.

Imagine the people of God, escaping Egypt, pursued by Pharaoh's army, trapped on all sides, when suddenly the Red Sea opened up and allowed them to cross to safety on the other side. Then envision their glee as the waters closed up again, to bury the Egyptian army. Quite an experience!

Please notice, however, that they didn't build a monument there, and spend the rest of their lives talking about their amazing "God moment." No, after Miriam composed a song and they took a few minutes to celebrate the mighty victory, they moved on. They took this miracle as evidence that God was with them, and would be with them every step of the way. In fact, it *launched* them on their way to the Promised Land.

Similarly, when the disciples saw Jesus ascend toward heaven and disappear in a cloud, they didn't stay there. In fact, a messenger from heaven appeared and told them to get busy with the assignment they had been given.

Fast forward to the day of Pentecost, when the Holy Spirit was poured out, as Jesus had said would happen. The disciples didn't get stuck in that marvelous, life-shaking moment, but rather allowed the experience to propel them forward to influence their world for Christ.

As Jesus had said, "…In a few days you will be baptized with the Holy Spirit. But you will receive power when the Holy Spirit comes on you; and you will be my witnesses in Jerusalem, and in all Judea and Samaria, and to the ends of the earth" (Acts 1:4-5, 8, NIV).

Thank the Lord for His work in our lives, and the many experiences we may have on our journey with Him. But the question we must ask is, "Does an experience grab our attention away for the assignment we have been given, or does it initiate energy and incentive to fulfill the Great Commission?"

Point People to Jesus

This is what our life is to be about.

Do we want to walk in the fullness of the Holy Spirit? Absolutely! And if we are truly walking in His fullness, we'll be looking more like Him every day. Our lives will reflect the fruit of the Spirit: love, joy, peace, patience, kindness, gentleness, goodness, faithfulness, and self control.

That kind of life will definitely point people toward Jesus.

I was riding my motorcycle recently, focused on the road ahead, when I approached a crossroads. Easing off on the throttle, I took note of a small sign pointing to the left that said, "Broadview." Another sign, pointing to the right, said "Laurel." The road was clearly marked and the signs fulfilled their function. You could turn onto one of those roads and know exactly where you would end up.

May our lives that clearly point people to Jesus.

Open Yourself to All of the Truth of Scripture

Because Thomas Jefferson didn't believe in the miracles of the Bible, he had a version published that removed the miraculous.

I haven't visited a Christian bookstore for awhile, but I just don't remember seeing the "Thomas Jefferson Study Bible" on the shelves. I have a feeling it was never very popular. Imagine taking a pair of scissors and cutting out sections of the Bible you didn't think should be there, wish weren't there, or disagreed with. How much would be left?

One evening I sat with a group of deacons from the church we attended at the time. We had a disagreement about our beliefs concerning the Holy Spirit, and were attempting to talk it through and come to some consensus.

One of the men picked up my New Testament that was on the coffee table, and began thumbing through it. I'd been doing a study on the Holy Spirit, and had marked every reference to the Holy Spirit with a blue pencil.

As he quickly glanced through the pages and saw all that blue, he looked up and said, "If I marked all those passages in my Bible, I might believe what you do."

I'm afraid that my immaturity and lack of the fruit of the Spirit were obvious at that point. I said, "Would you like to borrow my Bible?"

It may not have been the wisest, most gracious thing to say, but the point remains: Let's not cut out sections of the Bible, but rather seek to understand it as best we can, and then go out and live by it.

Granted, many things that have happened in the name of the Holy Spirit are, in reality, the work of human flesh. But let's not allow the way some people have misrepresented the Spirit to intimidate us from walking in the fullness of what God has for us.

Wait for the Gift Jesus Promised

"I am going to send you what my Father has promised; but stay in the city until you have been clothed with power from on high" (Luke 24:49, NIV)

On a cold Montana winter morning, I scraped ice off the windshield on my SUV, climbed in, and turned the key in the ignition…only to hear that tell-tale click. The battery was completely dead.

I got out of the car, frustrated. On some frigid winter days, everything seems inconvenient. But I was encouraged when I heard the sound of another vehicle slowly moving behind me, down the street.

I hurriedly ran after the vehicle and waved down the driver. He rolled down his window as he was backing up.

"Would you mind giving me a jump start?" I asked. Montana people are generally very nice and helpful...and most everyone carries jumper cables in the wintertime.

"Of course," the driver said, and pulled his truck up beside my Yukon. A few minutes later my SUV was purring, and the heater was warming my frozen feet. I had power!

One of the purposes of the Holy Spirit is to give us power to be an influence for Jesus. Jesus told the disciples to go and influence their world, but then said, "Wait, you need power."[30]

Expect to be a Witness for Jesus

"But you will receive power when the Holy Spirit comes on you; and you will be my witnesses in Jerusalem, and in all Judea and Samaria, and to the ends of the earth. (Acts 1:8, NIV)

"Always be prepared to give an answer to everyone who asks you to give the reason for the hope that you have. But do this with gentleness and respect." (1 Peter 3:15, NIV)

To be a valid witness for Jesus, we need His power. And it would also be helpful if we had something meaningful to say!

I would encourage you to take a few minutes, sit down, and write out the story of how you came to be a follower of Christ. As 1 Peter 3:15 communicates, you should always be ready to share your faith.

Include in your story these simple elements:

What was your life like before Christ?

What happened when you put your faith in Jesus? How has your life changed?

Then, please, memorize your story, rehearse it several times, and be prepared to share it in three minutes or less. You never, never know when the opportunity will arise.

There are many helpful tools to help you share your faith. I encourage you to find some that suit you and make them your own. Always be prepared!

Jesus gave us a clear assignment, and He also made it clear that He would always be there to help us fulfill that assignment. He clearly said, "Go and make disciples of all nations." But then, in the very next breath, He said, "Surely I am with you always, to the very end of the age." (Matthew 28:19, 20)

Chapter Eight

Don't Get Stuck in the Huddle

As a big fan of college basketball, I'm blessed to live in a city with two small colleges that always put good teams on the court. Because I want to be as close to the action as possible, I have season tickets, right behind the home team bench.

From my privileged perch, I'm only a few feet away from the coach and players. When the coach calls a timeout, I feel like I'm pretty much in the huddle, and can see everything that's going on, just a few feet away. Whether it's a thirty-second or a full time-out, the coach is usually talking furiously. Sometimes he's intense, at other times he's calm; but he's always teaching. Often, he is handed a clipboard, with a diagram of the basketball court printed on it. He takes his marker and draws up the next play.

At a recent game, I watched attentively as the coach worked with his players during a timeout late in the second overtime. You could feel the tension throughout the whole gym, but the intensity in the huddle was electric.

My eyes were fixed on the coach, as he looked around the huddle at each player.

"Isn't this great?" he said with a broad grin on his face. "This is why I coach, for times like this!" You could feel the pressure subside in the huddle, as he drew the next play on his clipboard.

Huddles in a basketball game have a purpose. They are for rest, instruction, and encouragement. Oftentimes the best-laid plans and purposes go awry, and players huddle up for fresh strategies to meet unanticipated needs. As crucial as these timeouts may be, however, no one buys a ticket to a basketball game to watch the huddle for two hours. It's a preposterous notion.

I propose that is exactly what many followers of Christ do: they get stuck in the huddle. In a basketball game, there are a limited number of timeouts allowed—only so many huddles. Perhaps churches would be well advised to devise such a rule for Christ-followers. After all, the church doesn't exist simply for "the huddle," or for gathering times. But gathering times are for the purpose of preparing us to do what Jesus told us to do.

And Jesus was very clear on what we are to be about.

One Unmistakable Syllable

"Therefore go and make disciples of all nations, baptizing them in the name of the Father and the Son and the Holy Spirit." [31]

"Go into all the world and preach the good news to all creation." [32]

The assignment Jesus gave his church is clear: "Go!"

In light of our assignment, the way so many people think about the church is interesting. For example, we say on Sunday morning, "Let's go to church."

Now don't get me wrong—I'm a church guy. But the huddle, church services, are only a small part of what the church is about.

The church gathers for the purpose of worship, rest, instruction, and encouragement. There is no question whether being together is a good thing, or a needed thing. In fact, God told us we should be together.

"Let us not give up meeting together, as some are in the habit of doing..." [33]

The implication of this verse is that some folks are prone to not huddle at all. Clearly, Scripture says this sort of isolationism is wrong.

Some folks, however, seem to huddle all the time. That's what they do. That's what Christianity is to them: huddling with other followers of Christ. They have forgotten that the huddle, times of gathering, are for the purpose of helping us prepare to fulfill our God given assignment.

"Go!"

A Heritage of Huddling

While I greatly value my Christian heritage and

don't want to sound critical…it sure seems like we huddled a lot when I was growing up.

We went to church every Sunday morning. There was no room for debate in this issue. In fact, we went to Sunday school, and then morning worship and Bible study.

On a normal Sunday after church we would go home for a nice dinner, then rest in the afternoon. But occasionally we went for a huddle at someone's house, better known as "fellowship."

In the evening we went to Training Union (a bit like Sunday school, only in the evening) followed by the Sunday evening service. And that was often followed by a huddle at someone's home for some more fellowship.

Wednesday evenings we huddled again for prayer and Bible study.

That was pretty much the norm for me and my family while I was growing up. We learned a lot, spent a lot of time together, and formed some great friendships—primarily with other Christ-followers.

We definitely knew how to huddle.

When I became a follower of Christ in my mid-twenties, I continued in the same pattern that had been modeled for me. Then, when I began leading a church in my early thirties, guess what we did? Huddle, huddle, huddle.

As a pastor, I consider myself a spiritual coach…and I truly love what I do: leading people into a deeper personal relationship with Christ and one another. I have devoted most of my adult life to these endeavors.

As the church I lead began to grow, however, the responsibilities of family, leading a church, and all that goes with that—counseling, preparing three messages a week, and preaching six times a week—began to wear me down. Fatigue forced me to seriously evaluate the pace of my life. At the same time, I took a look at those I was leading, and at what I was asking *them* to do.

It was then I realized that we were so busy with Christian activities we didn't have time to do what Jesus asked us to do: "Go!"

As a result, I began to give myself, and those I lead, a break. Intentionally, we began to meet less often, so people had the opportunity to "go" and be an influence in the lives of others.

Imagine a basketball team circled around the coach, in a huddle. The referee walks toward them and shouts a reminder, "It's time to break!" The coach steps out of the circle, the players reach toward the center of the huddle and join hands, and shout in unison "Go team!"

They then proceed to do what they have been trained to do, play basketball. They take the plays drawn up on chalkboards and whiteboards and tablets and make them come alive in the battle at hand.

It's not about the huddle, as necessary as that may be. The goal isn't huddling, the goal is getting into the game.

What does "getting in the game" mean for you and me? Bottom line, it means allowing your life to be an influence for the Lord Jesus in the world around you—by example, by attitude, and by spoken word.

Here are just a few ideas to that end....

Join an organization where you'll meet pre-Christians

Being in the grocery business for a number of years afforded me many good opportunities to be around pre-Christians every day—sales people, customers, vendors, and employees. Over the years, I'm grateful to say, the Lord used me to be an influence in the lives of many of those people I worked with.

During that same timeframe, I joined the local Rotary Club. What an opportunity that afforded to develop friendships, as we met each week!

In recent years, I accepted a position on a hospital board. Frankly, the business we accomplish isn't what gives meaning to my experience. It's the friendships that have developed.

I now belong to a local golf club. I love to golf and take advantage of the many opportunities of being part of that organization, but I also take pleasure in the opportunity to meet people who are not yet followers of Christ.

What about you? Look around. There must be similar opportunities for you to get involved in the lives of people. Be secure in the fact that Jesus has prepared you—and them!—for meaningful encounters. Don't miss the opportunity.

Recognize your propensity to get comfortable

The easy path is to gravitate toward relationships with other Christ-followers—people with values similar to our own, a lifestyle we can appreciate, and a belief system consistent with ours.

In other words, people a lot like us.

As a result, difficult conversations are minimized. Frankly, life is so full and pressure-filled that it's very easy to take the path of least resistance, and escape into our comfort zone. (Dare I say, "become *stuck* in our comfort zone"?)

Make no mistake. We certainly need supportive relationships with people we love and enjoy being around. But I encourage you not to allow yourself to gravitate toward those relationships *exclusively*.

Jesus was constantly stretching His disciples beyond their comfort zones, and He's doing the same thing today.

One evening, I was called to the hospital. An acquaintance had a family member who was dying. I knew the young woman who had called me quite well, but only knew her father-in-law by reputation. Quite frankly, it wasn't all that positive.

I walked into the hospital room, where family members were seated around the bed. The father-in-law was in a coma, and expected to die within hours. I turned to his daughter-in-law and asked, "How can I help you guys?"

I was actually thinking to myself, *This man is going to die. There's no hope for him, but perhaps I can be of some help to the family.*

The Lord had something else in mind. The young woman said to me, "Pastor, our dad is dying, and we want you to pray for him to come to know Jesus before he dies."

I was taken aback by her request. This was in the miracle realm, a domain I'm not that familiar with. In compliance with her request, however, I walked toward the bed, and placed my hand on the man's fore-head. I didn't pray all that loud, and I don't remember being particularly filled with faith. I only made this simple request: "Lord, this room is filled with people who love this man. Our prayer is that You would reveal Yourself to him in such a way that he could give his heart to You before he dies."

As I was praying, the man's eyes suddenly flew open. Lurching upright in bed, his face only inches from mine, his penetrating eyes fixed and focused on mine. Frankly, I was petrified.

He stared directly into my eyes for what seemed to be three or four minutes. It was probably three or four seconds, but that's a long time when a dead man is staring you down.

He didn't say anything, he only stared. Then he laid back down and passed away a few hours later.

At his funeral a few days later, I told the story of what had taken place in the hospital room. The family and others who had gathered were deeply encouraged by God's commitment to reveal Himself to this man. Was he saved in those moments? Only God knows. But we do know that something supernatural took place at a very opportune time.

Now, looking back, how does that experience look to me on balance? Let's see…we have my discomfort on one side, and a man's eternity on the other. Hmmm. The fact is, I *like* being comfortable, and I suspect you do as well. But when I have the opportunity to make a difference in someone's forever, I'll take it!

Enjoy the company of selected pre-Christians

Hanging out with people who are not yet Christ-followers can get a little sticky at times. This is one of those things, of course, for which Jesus was so roundly criticized by the religious elite. They sneered at Him for being "a friend of sinners."[34]

The difficulty lies in the fact that some people use this as an excuse to go back to their old lifestyles, hanging out in places they shouldn't be, doing things they shouldn't be doing.

It's always wise to remember why we are developing a friendship with someone who is not yet a Christ follower, and ask our self, "Who is influencing whom?" If we are being influenced rather than being an influence, we may want to evaluate: "Is this the right person for me to be with?"

Remember, we can't influence everyone, but we can influence someone. So the question is, "Whom has Jesus placed in your life, at this point in time, that you can influence in positive and healthy ways for His sake?"

On several occasions, I have developed intentional relationships through racquetball, or golf. Many years ago, a woman in the church was very concerned about the spiritual life of her husband. Knowing he liked racquetball, I called him and asked if he would like to join me for a match at the YMCA. He agreed, and over the course of time a friendship began to develop.

We played racquetball once or twice a week for over a year. Eventually, he began attending church, and ultimately gave his life to Christ. He remains a follower of Christ to this day.

I love making friends with store clerks, waiters, and waitresses. The relationship may not go deep, but at least it's an opportunity to make a positive impression as a follower of Christ. They've probably had enough negative examples.

One of my daughters is outstanding at building these kinds of friendships. She befriends these people in the marketplace, builds trust with them, gives them gifts, buys them flowers…whatever it takes. Then, at the opportune time, she invites them to church with her. And they come! What an influence!

Ask God to place people in your path

And be prepared for God to answer this request quickly!

I had just gotten comfortable on a plane when a young woman tapped me on the shoulder and asked if I would mind scooting over one seat. She said, "My friend is seated across the aisle and we would love to be able to visit."

I told her I would be glad to move, and did. Once again I settled in, and slipped off into an enjoyable, though brief, afternoon nap.

When I woke up, the young woman was sitting quietly next to me. She noticed I was awake, and asked, "Where are you going?" I told her I was headed for Palm Springs.

"You must be on vacation," she said.

"No," I replied, "I'm actually going there to work."

Then came the question I always look forward to. "What do you do?" she asked. I leaned toward her a bit, looked at her out of the corner of my eye, and said,

"I'm a pastor."

Her response came sooner and more exuberantly than I had ever experienced when asked that question.

"I can't believe this! I can't *believe* this!" she said, obviously elated.

I smiled. "Why is that?"

"I just can't believe this!" she said again. I was just sitting here thinking to myself, "God, if You are there and You care about what is going on in my life, please reveal Yourself to me some way."

And then she concluded, "And here I am sitting next to a priest!"

I chuckled, and sat up in my seat. It was obvious an opportunity had just been presented to me by the Lord.

She went on to say, "I wasn't even supposed to be on this plane. I missed my flight last night, and got put on standby today. I wasn't supposed to be in this seat; I was back there. But here I am, sitting next to you." It was very clear to her that God had answered her prayer.

We talked for a few minutes, then she sat quietly for a bit. I was astounded at her next comment, "Do you suppose God could ever forgive me for all the things I've done?" Talk about an open door! I had one!

Just before we landed, I handed her a card with my contact information. I've never heard from her, but I'm very confident that I was used by the Lord to nudge her a bit closer to crossing the line of faith.

So whom has God placed in your path?

Allow me to be your coach for a moment. We've been huddled for a few minutes—me writing, you reading. Now it's time to get in the game. I'm going to step out of the huddle. Will you? Take a risk, step up, get out of the huddle and into the game!

Chapter Nine

Unstuck:
Life with a Purpose

One night after a midweek service, I drove out of the parking lot of Beaverton Foursquare Church, in Beaverton, Oregon, where the late Dr. Ron Mehl was pastor. While we were in church, there had been an ice storm. These are fairly common in the Northwest; it's just cold enough for the rain to turn to ice when it hits the ground.

As you can well imagine, however, this sudden layer of ice over everything creates some particularly treacherous driving conditions. As I approached the freeway ramp to head toward downtown Portland, I noticed a number of cars stopped in front of me—some turned sideways, some backwards, and some in the ditch.

All stuck. All going nowhere. And I was about to join them.

It was then that I saw the four-wheel drive pickup with a winch on the front. I watched the owner of the pickup as he approached one car after another. He would speak to the driver of the car for a few seconds, then attach a cable to the bumper of their car and pull it up the hill and onto the freeway. They were on their way at last, unstuck.

Finally it was my turn. The man walked up to my window and asked me if I would like a tow. "Of course," I said. I was a bit shocked when he quickly fired back, "That'll be ten dollars."

He must have made four hundred bucks that night by helping people like me get unstuck and on our way to our destinations. When you think about it, the services he provided would have been quite a bargain at twice the price!

In our brief time together within these pages, I have offered a number of suggestions on how you might get unstuck and remain so. I want to conclude our time together by reminding you how valuable you are to God, and how committed He is to your continued progress in moving toward the destiny He has for you.

There is a question that is asked frequently around my house: *"Where's my purse?"* Ginger seems to ask that question every time we're about to head out the door.

I call it "the eternal question."

If I'm upstairs, she calls out, "Is my purse up there?" If I'm downstairs, it's, "Is my purse down there?" Upstairs or downstairs, inside or outside, we frequently find ourselves in the purse-location business.

Why? Because it's important. Ginger's purse is valuable to Ginger, and Ginger is valuable to me. It's a privilege to look for that purse. If I ever lost my wallet, it would be the same, with roles reversed. The fact is, when something valuable to us is lost, we look for it, even pursue it.

As incredible as it sounds, that's how the great God and Creator of the universe views you and me: *valuable.* So much so that in Jesus' own words, He came to "seek and save what was lost." [35] Envision it if you can....You are so valuable to God that He sent His only Son to get you unstuck and on your way to becoming everything He purposed for you. He did so through the ultimate sacrifice, giving up His own life.

There are many biblical examples of God helping people get unstuck. He didn't let Abraham remain stuck; He fulfilled His promise and gave Abraham a son. He didn't let Jacob remained stuck in a foreign land, in subservience to Laban; He brought Jacob back to his homeland. He didn't let Joseph remained stuck in Egypt alone; Joseph's relationship with his family was restored. He didn't allow David to remain stuck in sin; he sent Nathan to help set him free. He didn't allow Peter to remain stuck in shame after he denied Jesus; He restored him to fellowship and renewed his commission to serve.

And by the way, He doesn't want you to remain stuck at any point in your life, either. In fact, He has infinite resources to pull you out of where you shouldn't be and get you back on the road to purpose, contentment, and great joy.

My hope in offering this little book to you is, first of all, to help you get unstuck. But equally important is that your freedom would be followed by the recognition that Jesus is asking people who know Him—people like you—to move toward helping others out of the ditch. Remembering that Jesus paid the ultimate price for our freedom, His own life, the least we can do is give of our time and energy and compassion to help others experience the same freedom we enjoy.

Most of us, at one time or another in our lives, have felt a real reluctance to "get involved" in the life of another. The most common reaction I've gotten when I've urged people in this direction is much like Moses' response when he was asked by God to help the Hebrews get unstuck.

Moses said, "Who am I?"

It seems most of us feel a bit inadequate when God nudges us toward reaching out a hand to help someone else. I heard a beautiful little story a few years ago that may prove helpful in overcoming your hesitancy.[36]

A man who was a believer was headed for the airport to catch a plane. He was late, and feared being bumped from the flight. When he arrived, however, he was quite relieved to find he still had a spot on the plane. But it wasn't the spot he wanted. He was now in a middle seat—the very place he had hoped to avoid.

As he buckled up, he noticed a Down's syndrome girl on one side of him, and a well-dressed businessman on the other. The girl was delightful; she looked at him, face beaming, grinning from ear to ear. He smiled back, greeted her, and quickly grabbed a magazine to pass the time.

After a few moments, she nudged him. As he turned to look her way she asked him a rather politically-incorrect question, "Did you brush your teeth this morning?"

A bit taken aback, he hesitated for a moment, but then replied, "Why, yes, I did."

"Well, that's good," she replied. "People should brush their teeth every day."

He agreed, in a matter-of-fact tone, "Yes they should."

They smiled at each other, and he turned his eyes back toward the magazine he had been reading.

A few moments later, she nudged him again, probing a bit further, "Do you smoke?"

He chuckled to himself, and then told her, "No, I don't smoke."

She was obviously pleased with his response and replied, "That's good, because people who smoke die."

He smiled, acknowledged his agreement, and resumed reading his magazine.

He wasn't so surprised the third nudge came along. But he was pleasantly caught off guard by her next question. "Do you love Jesus?" she asked sincerely.

Now he beamed. "Yes, I do!" he said. "In fact, I have dedicated my life to serve Him." Their friendship was now sealed; she knew she had a friend.

"That's *good!*" she affirmed, with enthusiastic support for his faith in Christ.

She then turned her attention toward the well-dressed businessman who was seated by the aisle, one seat over from her new-found friend. The businessman had been busily working on his laptop, apparently oblivious to the conversation that had just taken place.

She leaned over and whispered to her friend, in the middle seat, "Ask him if he brushed his teeth this morning," she instructed.

So he leaned over and quietly said to the busy businessman, "Excuse me sir. My little friend here would like to know if you brushed your teeth this morning."

You can guess how the conversation progressed. When she determined the businessman brushed his teeth and didn't smoke, she followed up with, "Ask him if he loves Jesus."

Her friend in the middle seat passed on the question. She watched expectantly as the businessman hesitated for a moment, then said, "You know, I've been wondering about Him." For the next hour and a half, a delightful exchange took place between the two men.

This young lady had a purpose in life, and was determined to be about it. How about you? Now that we've completed our time together, my prayer for you is that you will remain unstuck and confident in God's commitment that you remain so. I also pray that you will have the dedication and courage to be used by God to help others who may be stuck.

I'll tell you right up front—it's not a life for the faint of heart. Perhaps you've seen the photograph of the construction workers sitting together on a steel girder, hundreds of feet above the streets of New York City, comfortably having lunch together. Undoubtedly, at one point in each of their lives, such heights terrified them.

I challenge you to live a courageous life with God by your side, helping you remain unstuck and helping you assist others on their journey.

"Have I not commanded you? Be strong and courageous. Do not be terrified; do not be discouraged, for the LORD your God will be with you wherever you go." (Joshua 1:9 (NIV)

May God give you grace in your journey!

1. 1 Samuel 17:45
2. Jeremiah 1:5
3. Jeremiah 1:6
4. Jeremiah 1:7
5. Isaiah 41:10
6. James 4:6
7. 2 Kings 5
8. Proverbs 8:13
9. Psalm 138:6
10. Matthew 26:31-46
11. Luke 14:7-10
12. John 9:39
13. Acts 8:14-17
14. Matthew 13:1-23
15. Proverbs 17:28
16. Luke 10:41
17. Luke 12:15
18. James 1:14-15
19. Matthew 13:22
20. Matthew 13:22
21. Merriam Webster's Dictionary, tenth edition.
22. Matthew 19:16-29
23. Matthew 19:21
24. Matthew 19:22
25. Matthew 19:27
26. Matthew 19:29
27. Matthew 6:19-21
28. Matthew 6:26-27, 32
29. Warren Wiersbe, The Bible Exposition Commentary.
30. Luke 24:46-49
31. Matthew 28:19
32. Mark 16:15
33. Hebrews 10:25
34. Matthew 11:19
35. Luke 19:10
36. Source unknown